mandela

ECHOES OF AN ERA BY **ALF KUMALO**
TEXT BY　　　　　**ES'KIA MPHAHLELE**

mandELA
ECHOES OF AN ERA

PENGUIN BOOKS

PENGUIN BOOKS

Published by the Penguin Group
27 Wrights Lane, London w8 5TZ, England
Viking Penguin Inc, 40 West 23rd Street, New York, New York 10010, USA
Penguin Books Australia Ltd, Ringwood, Victoria, Australia
Penguin Books Canada Ltd, 2801 John Street, Markham, Ontario, Canada LR3 1B4
Penguin Books (NZ) Ltd, 182-190 Wairau Road, Auckland 10, New Zealand
Penguin Books, Amethyst Street, Theta Ext 1, Johannesburg, South Africa

Penguin Books Ltd, Registered Offices: Harmondsworth, Middlesex, England

First published in 1990 by Penguin Books, South Africa

ISBN 0 14 0143165

Designed and produced by
Press Books, P O Box 33414, Jeppestown, Johannesburg 2000
Positives by H A Litho
Printed and bound by Interpak

f o r e WORD

The story of Nelson Mandela's life is intertwined with an account of forty-one years of the African National Congress's history. It is a story of a leadership of the ANC which found itself changing its stance and political style from time to time. It is the story of a national movement that was silenced early in its life, from 1960 when it was banned.

But the narrative between the covers of this book, pictorial and verbal, is a record not only of a public figure and his political struggle, but also a man who experienced personal tragedy, including the death of a son.

Above all this, however, towers the figure of a man who has at all times shown innate qualities of leadership, which have never been allowed to be tested.

Photographer Alf Kumalo and Es'kia Mphahlele have put together a telling tribute to Nelson Mandela, and a timely one. This book appears at a time when Mandela has finally been brought back, so to speak, onto the mainland of human affairs, brought there by the huge tidal wave of history. The pressure brought to bear on the Government from among us the oppressed and from abroad has in an uncanny way brought us back full circle: the announcement of the lifting of legal restrictions, the unbanning of the PAC, ANC and SA Communist Party ... It seems like only yesterday, but in reality such a long, aching 26 years ago, we were saying bitter, angry, tearfilled farewells to our families and friends when we were sentenced to life imprisonment in 1964.

And now begins the next chapter of the struggle for total liberation.

The book presents the essentials; it reflects, in pictures and in text, Mandela's life and times. All else might be seen as peripheral, and Es'kia says if he were writing a novel, he would give particular attention to those very elements we might regard as peripheral, because, he explains, "that in reality is where several other lives lurk: the ghosts and shades, the loves and hates, the suspicions and obsessions, the doubts, the private confessions".

The Kumalo-Mphahlele stage teems with actors, but of necessity the most prominent of these remain longer under the narrative spotlight as the course of our political resistance is traced from its beginnings.

The photographs bear witness to those other no less prominent names and events which came to the fore while Mandela and his comrades were imprisoned.

This is indeed a chronicle that measures up to the stature of its chief actor, Nelson Mandela.

In 1959 the Transvaal African Teachers' Association (TATA), in collaboration with the Cape Town-based Teachers' League of South Africa (TLSA), launched a campaign against Bantu Education and a system that was being proposed especially for the "Coloureds".

A report had been published that year by a commission of inquiry headed by Dr W W M Eiselen. The commission's recommendation, among other things, aimed at lowering the standards and quality of education for Africans. The Minister of Native Affairs, H F Verwoerd, was to tell the House of Assembly in 1953 (the year Bantu Education became an Act):

When I have control of Native education I will reform it so that Natives will be taught from childhood to realize that equality with Europeans is not for them ... People who believe in equality are not desirable teachers for natives. When my department controls Native education it will know for what class of higher education the Native is fitted, and whether he will have a chance in life to use his knowledge.

The 1951 campaigns launched by the teachers' organisations were precisely in anticipation of the law — one that moulded the evil system still with us today.

An early picture of Nelson Mandela, aged 24, seen here with photographs of Chief Jongintaba, paramount chief of the Tembus and the man who brought him up.

In the 1950s, despite vigorous protest from its inhabitants, Sophiatown was razed to the ground. Home to a mix of many South African communities, the township was regarded by the Nationalist Government as an offensive blot on the pure map of apartheid. Many political meetings, such as the ones pictured here, took place in protest against the peoples' forced removal, but to no avail. Today nothing remains of Sophiatown's colour and flamboyance. In its place stands a neat white suburb of Johannesburg — its name: Triomf.

Six years later, in 1959, a member of parliament was to say, "The Bantu must be so educated that they do not want to become imitators [of Whites, but] that they will want to remain essentially Bantu."

Back to 1951. This writer, then general secretary of the TATA, together with its president, Zeph Mothopeng (later to become a Robben Islander, subsequently to become president of the Pan-Africanist Congress), went to consult a neighbour of high rank in the African National Congress and president of the Youth League about the Eiselen

report. This neighbour happened to be Nelson Mandela, living a few blocks away, in Orlando West.

We asked Mr Mandela if the ANC could give the TATA a national platform from which to address larger audiences to alert them against the imminent onslaught on the African children's minds through Bantu Education: a matter of great national importance. The Eiselen report was certain to be translated into an Act of Parliament. One of the recommendations of the

Commission was that Africans should be taught in the medium of the mother-tongue throughout their school life. This meant at least six languages. It also meant that the Nationalist Government was determined to kill ideas, which came to us in English, if the latter was going to be suppressed. Mandela told us that education was not a priority. National liberation was. Education could receive attention after liberation.

When the Bantu Education Act broke upon us in 1953, needless to say, the ANC leadership were

"I HATE RACIAL DISCRIMINATION MOST INTENSELY AND IN ALL ITS MANIFESTA- TIONS. I HAVE FOUGHT IT ALL MY LIFE. I FIGHT IT NOW. I DETEST MOST INTENSELY THE SET-UP THAT SURROUNDS ME HERE. IT MAKES ME FEEL THAT I AM A BLACK MAN IN A WHITE MAN'S COURT. THIS SHOULD NOT BE." — M A N D E L A

◄ Albertina Sisulu and Winnie Mandela pictured together in tribal dress, 1959. Albertina Sisulu, one of three elected presidents of the UDF, and wife of Walter Sisulu, former Secretary General of the ANC, has long been a vociferous campaigner against apartheid. Banned or restricted on and off for more than 17 years, she never gave up the struggle and addressed political rallies and meetings at every opportunity.

caught with their pants down. There were hurried, desperate directives for the masses to boycott the law by pulling
their children out of the schools, which were from then on
going to be under State control. Half-hearted and feeble
efforts were made to teach cultural and political awareness
in independent schools. The children returned to formal
schooling. Several teachers, however, were fired for their
sympathies with the ANC, but not before this writer, Mothopeng and a third official of TATA, I. Mathlare, had been
axed. We were fired in 1952.

Mandela soon realised that the cultural front, including
education, could not be neglected in the totality of the
political struggle. No doubt the ANC had too many other
issues to attend to in 1951 which it considered claimed
precedence. The previous year there had been a fatal
mixup in the relations between the ANC Youth League and
the Communist Party (CP). The Party had sent out a call for
workers to stop work on May 1, to protest the banning of its
members — Y Dadoo, J B Marks and Moses Kotane.
Despite the ANC's objection to the stayaway, several

Downtown Johannesburg,
1958. Two black youths arrested.
Many such children roamed the city's
streets.

10

Nelson and Winnie Mandela were married in Bizana in 1958 in this unpretentious church. At the time, Nelson was involved in the famous Treason Trial and had to apply for his restriction order to be lifted in order to travel to the Transkei for his marriage.

workers obeyed the stoppage call. Lives were lost during a confrontation with the police.

Walter Sisulu, secretary of the Youth League-controlled ANC since 1949, had called the Executive Committee together (including Oliver Tambo and Mandela) to discuss methods of protest against the killings and injuries unleashed by the police. The ANC and its Youth League, with the South African Indian Congress, forged a truce with the CP. The Suppression of Communism Act, the Group Areas Act, which legislated the geographical and social separation of the races, the Population Registration Act, which fenced in the races according to colour and biological discrimination — all these weighed heavily on the minds of the ANC leaders in 1951. Added to this, preparations were afoot for the next year's Defiance Campaign against Unjust Laws — acts of civil disobedience. Mandela was to be volunteer-in-chief, with Maulvi Cachalia of the Indian Congress as his assistant.

◄■ Nelson Mandela and Ruth First after the 1961 Treason Trial. First was a steadfast opponent of the policies of apartheid. In 1949 she married Joe Slovo, a leading figure at the time in the Congress of Democrats. She left South Africa for Maputo in Mozambique, where she worked for the African National Congress. On 17 August 1982 she received a parcel which came by post. It exploded in her hands and she was killed.

More immediately, when Mandela passed that verdict about education in 1951, the Youth League was engaged in a joint effort with the Indian Congress to organise a nationwide stoppage of work on June 26.

Indeed the 1950s were a decade of lofty idealism among the ANC mass movement and the leadership. Freedom seemed just around the corner. Hence the belief that political hardships could first be parcelled up in one bundle and buried in a bottomless pit; clear the decks, so to speak,

"THE CHARTER IS MORE THAN A MERE LIST OF DEMANDS FOR DEMOCRATIC REFORMS. IT IS A REVOLUTIONARY DOCUMENT PRECISELY BECAUSE THE CHANGES IT ENVISAGES CANNOT BE WON WITHOUT BREAKING UP THE ECONOMIC AND POLITICAL SET-UP OF PRESENT SOUTH AFRICA. TO WIN THE DEMANDS CALLS FOR THE ORGANISATION, LAUNCHING AND DEVELOPMENT OF MASS STRUGGLE ON THE WIDEST SCALE." — M A N D E L A

◄▌ Nelson and Winnie Mandela at the conclusion of the Treason Trial, 1961. This was a farcical, time consuming and expensive trial which began on 5 December 1956, when 156 persons from various parts of and organisations in South Africa were arrested and held on charges of conspiracy and high treason. Among prominent activists arrested were Nobel Peace Prizewinner Albert Lutuli, president-general of the ANC, Monty Naicker, president of the Natal Indian Congress and the venerable Prof Z K Matthews, vice-principal of Fort Hare. By March 1961, the charges having failed to be substantiated, all the trialists had been acquitted.

before education could claim our attention. While mass rally after mass rally during the decade seemed to inflate the euphoria of black people under the banner of the Congress Alliance, police were becoming more vigilant, more ruthless in their methods of breaking up meetings.

The 1952 campaign of civil disobedience, launched on June 26, was one such big rally to test the political muscle of the Congress Alliance for the first time. It was conceived in the spirit of Mahatma Gandhi's satyagraha — passive resistance. Some 8,500 volunteers were arrested. Mandela, then president of the Transvaal ANC, Dr James S Moroka, the national president, and secretary Sisulu were among those prosecuted under the Suppression of Communism Act. Although the trial was the State's immediate response to the Defiance Campaign, the Act itself was retroactive in effect.

◖◣ Walter Sisulu (centre) and others discuss the outcome at the end of the Treason Trial.

◀ Joe Slovo, already a banned person at the time of the Treason Trial, Advocate Duma Nokwe and Ellen Bernstein discuss the verdict at the Drill Hall. Advocate Nokwe, acting Secretary-General of the African National Congress, was also one of the accused and had an opportunity to address the court.

 Nelson Mandela leads the people in song at the conclusion of the Treason Trial.

Dr Moroka sought a separate trial, to everyone's dismay. The decision killed his political career, or what there was of it in the first place. Chief Albert Lutuli succeeded him in that year. Mandela and Sisulu were among the 52 to be banned in December of 1952, after all the accused had received suspended sentences.

The euphoria released by the very act of defiance in the campaign is reflected in Mandela's presidential address "No Easy Walk to Freedom" (1953). The title came from a phrase in one of Pundit Nehru's books: "We held the initiative and the forces of freedom were advancing on all fronts." He was further to caution:

Long speeches, the shaking of fists, the banging of tables, and strongly worded resolutions out of touch with conditions do not bring about mass action and can do a great deal of harm to the organization and the struggle we serve. We understood that the masses had to be made ready for the new forms of political struggle .... The old methods of bringing about mass action through public

 Defence lawyer Advocate Isaac Maisels celebrates the acquittal of the accused in the Treason Trial.

 Patrick Mulawa and congress organiser Steve Segale attending the Treason Trial. Ida Mntwana, member of the Youth League, looks on. Mulawa was later to die in combat, attempting to cross the border into South Africa. Segale was active in assisting Sophiatown residents at the time of their forced removal.

mass meetings, press statements and leaflets ... have become extremely dangerous and difficult to use effectively .... There is hardly a printing press which will agree to print leaflets calling upon workers to embark upon industrial action, for fear of prosecution .... These developments require the evolution of new forms of political struggle ... to strive for action on a higher level than the Defiance Campaign.

Even this criticism, sound as it was, was inspired by the idealism of the fifties rooted in the ANC style of open politics. The Special Branch knew every move the Congress Alliance was going to make, and forestalled it!

One of the "new forms" Mandela announced in the same address, read on his behalf, was a result of the decision taken jointly by the ANC and the South African Indian Congress (SAICC). It was known as the "M" Plan. Among the aims were "to enable the transmission of important decisions taken on a national level to every member of the organization without public meetings, issuing press statements and

Joe Slovo and Nelson

Mandela outside the courthouse.

"GOVERNMENT VIOLENCE CAN DO ONLY ONE THING AND THAT IS TO BREED COUNTER-VIOLENCE. WE HAVE WARNED REPEATEDLY THAT THE GOVERNMENT, BY RESORTING CONTINUALLY TO VIOLENCE, WILL BREED COUNTER-VIOLENCE AMONGST THE PEOPLE ..."

MANDELA   — PRETORIA COURT ADDRESS, NOVEMBER 1962

Nelson Mandela in thoughtful mood after his acquittal in the Treason Trial. One of his first actions after the trial was to organise a stay-away in protest against the Government's decision to declare South Africa a Republic.

printing circulars; to build up in the local branches themselves local congresses which will effectively represent the strength of the people; to extend and strengthen the ties between the Congress and the people and consolidate Congress leadership".

Mandela's first banning order expired in the same year (1953). He established his legal practice in partnership with Oliver Tambo. The Congress of Democrats (COD) was formed, representing the white-liberal front. It became the white wing of the Congress Alliance.

The climax of mass political consciousness and optimism was the Congress of the People which met on June 25, 1955 at Kliptown, Johannesburg. The Congress Alliance, including this time the South African Congress of Trade Unions, organised this mass rally — about 3 000 delegates from a diversity of organisations across the country. Banners screamed slogans such as FREEDOM IN OUR TIME

LONG LIVE THE STRUGGLE. A large green wheel of four spokes stood in the background, symbolising freedom: **25**

March 30, 1961. Jubilation on the faces of trialists and supporters as they drink milk to celebrate the end of the Treason Trial. Supporters and well-wishers would provide food and milk every day during breaks in the proceedings.

The early sixties were turbulent years in protest politics — the anti-pass law campaign, Sharpeville, the Treason Trial. Children's games in the townships reflected the mood of the times.

Mandela, looking relieved and relaxed after the trial.

ANC — African elephant; S A Indian Congress — Indian fox; S A Coloured People's Organization — "Coloured" horse; Congress of Democrats — European owl; and the S A Congress of Trade Unions which contained workers of all races.

This writer sat next to the Anglican activist priest, Fr Trevor Huddleston, C R, at the invitation of the planners to speak on Bantu Education. At one point a row of police sprang almost out of nowhere. They pointed their stenguns at us, a few centimetres from the tummy as we stood to sing the national anthems. Power demonstration, that's what the police were acting out. By then the Freedom Charter had been adopted to massive applause. This was a charter that was to represent the focus of ANC politics, to become a general framework for the kind of society the Alliance envisaged. The final charter was quite clearly the work of persons who wanted to avoid brazen fighting talk and also to reassure whites that their future was safe in South Africa.

In October of the same year, and under the leadership of Mrs Lilian Ngoye, the ANC Women's League organised a rally in which about 2 000 women converged on the Union

"THE WHOLE LIFE OF A THINKING AFRICAN IN THIS COUNTRY DRIVES HIM CONTINUOUSLY TO A CONFLICT BETWEEN HIS CONSCIENCE ON THE ONE HAND AND THE LAW ON THE OTHER ... THE CONFLICT ARISES FOR MEN OF CONSCIENCE, FOR MEN WHO THINK AND WHO FEEL DEEPLY IN EVERY COUNTRY."
— M A N D E L A

 Albertina Sisulu addresses a meeting of women in the 1960s. These women, called 'the suffering widows', were those whose husbands were gaoled or in detention at the time.

 Mandela, Winnie and their second daughter, Zindzi, photographed in 1961.

Buildings, Pretoria. They submitted a petition for the Prime Minister, J G Strijdom. Strijdom was one of the earliest in the line of hardline *verkramptes* to rule South Africa.

The women's song was a battlecry: "Strijdom, you have struck a rock once you have touched a woman!" In 1956 women were faced with the most humiliating experience: the order that they were from then on to carry passes, hitherto only a burden for males. This year also marks the beginning of the great Treason Trial. 156 ANC leaders sat in the dock. Clearly the Congress of the People had sent the shivers through Govern-

"WHILST THE CHARTER PROCLAIMS DEMOCRATIC CHANGES OF A FAR-REACHING NATURE, IT IS BY NO MEANS A BLUEPRINT FOR A SOCIALIST STATE BUT A PROGRAMME FOR THE UNIFICATION OF VARIOUS CLASSES AND GROUPINGS AMONGST THE PEOPLE ON A DEMOCRATIC BASIS."

MANDELA — *"IN OUR LIFETIME" LIBERATION* JUNE 1956

◄❚ Dr Nkomo, pictured in Soweto in 1962. Formerly active in the ANC, he subsequently became involved in the international movement Moral Rearmament.

◄❚ Winnie Mandela and Albertina Sisulu campaign for Mandela's release in 1962. Having been out of the country and travelling in Africa gaining support for the struggle, he secretly returned to South Africa but was arrested in Natal on 5 August. It was believed that police had been tipped off by an informer as to his whereabouts. Winnie herself was banned in 1962 for two years. In that year she was elected to the executive of the Federation of South African Women.

ment circles. The State was hellbent on making an example of the Congress Alliance leadership. The Freedom Charter, in spite of its mild and conciliatory tone, became the prime witness among the thousands of documents that were tabled. The charge was that between 1952 and 1956 the Congress Alliance had conspired to commit acts of sabotage and other forms of violence to overthrow the State. All the accused were acquitted, some earlier in the trial, the rest in 1961.

The year 1958 was a time of strife between the ANC

and an influential, highly vocal group of nationalists. They were a survival and extension of the earlier Youth League of the ANC. The origin of the League had been inspired in the late forties by a passionate love of motherland and the attitude that whites were of European descent, were intruders, colonisers and exploiters.

Under the leadership of Professor Mangaliso Sobukwe of the University of the Witwatersrand, Zeph

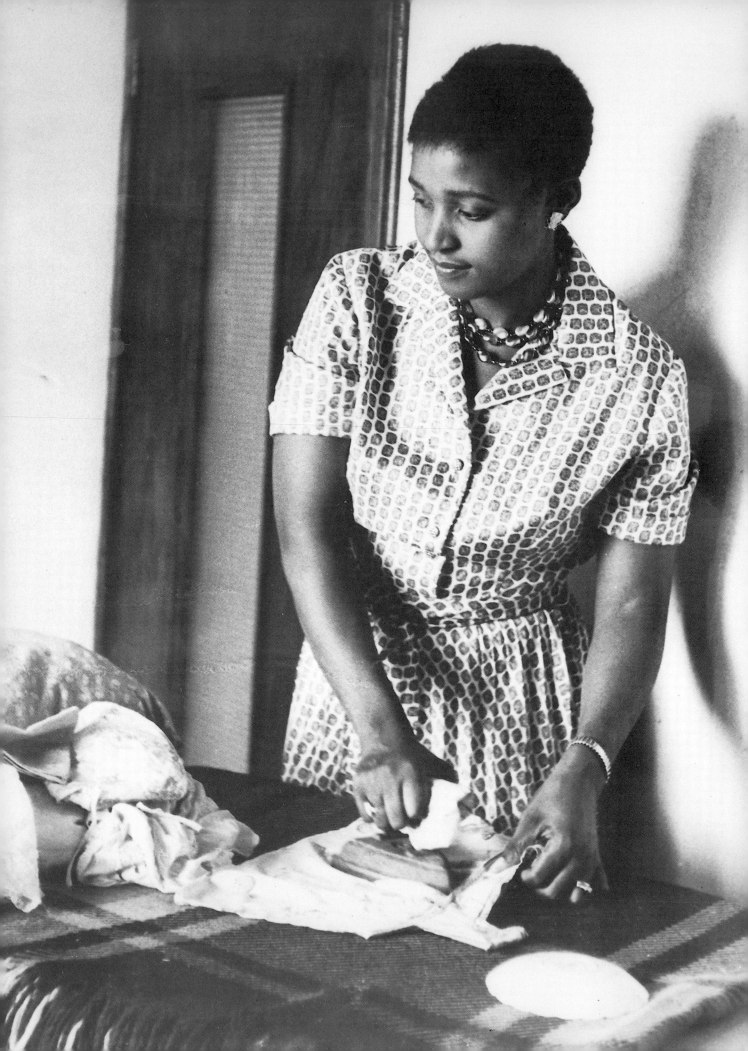

"WHEN A GOVERNMENT SEEKS TO SUPPRESS A PEACEFUL DEMONSTRATION OF AN UNARMED PEOPLE BY MOBILISING THE ENTIRE RESOURCES OF THE STATE, MILITARY AND OTHERWISE, IT CONCEDES POWERFUL MASS SUPPORT FOR SUCH A DEMONSTRATION. WE PLAN TO MAKE GOVERNMENT IMPOSSIBLE ...: I AM INFORMED THAT A WARRANT FOR MY ARREST HAS BEEN ISSUED AND THAT THE POLICE ARE LOOKING FOR ME ... [I] WILL NOT GIVE MYSELF UP TO A GOVERNMENT I DO NOT RECOGNISE."

M A N D E L A — PRESS STATEMENT RELEASED BY THE ALL-IN AFRICAN NATIONAL COUNCIL, JUNE 1961.

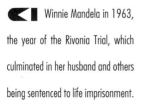 Winnie Mandela in 1963, the year of the Rivonia Trial, which culminated in her husband and others being sentenced to life imprisonment.

Mothopeng, Potlako Leballo, Peter Raboroko, J Madzunya and so on, the group broke away from the ANC in 1959 under the name Pan-Africanist Congress (PAC). The Africanists criticised the Freedom Charter for trying to accommodate whites. The African could not be expected to share the land with those who had "stolen" it from them ("The land shall belong to all who work it.") They saw the ANC as having abdicated its national-

ism and its leadership in favour of the white COD and CP who stayed underground.

The ANC and the PAC organised separate anti-pass campaigns. The PAC stronghold was in the Vaal Triangle and Cape Town. On March 21, 1960 the Sharpeville massacre broke upon us near Evaton. About 20 000 people had assembled under the PAC banner on an open plain to

Marcellino Dos Santos, pictured here in 1964 in Maputo, Mozambique.

33

"... IT WAS OUR INTENTION THAT THE DEMONSTRATION SHOULD GO THROUGH PEACEFULLY, WITHOUT CLASH OR CONFLICT, AS SUCH DEMONSTRATIONS DO IN EVERY CIVILISED COUNTRY. NEVERTHELESS, AROUND THAT CAMPAIGN AND OUR PREPARATIONS FOR THAT CAMPAIGN WAS CREATED THE ATMOSPHERE FOR CIVIL WAR AND REVOLUTION. I WOULD SAY DELIBERATELY CREATED. NOT BY US, YOUR WORSHIP, BUT BY THE GOVERNMENT, WHICH SET OUT ... TO REPRESENT US AS WILD, DANGEROUS REVOLUTIONARIES, INTENT ON DISORDER, AND RIOT."

MANDELA   — PRETORIA COURT ADDRESS, NOVEMBER 1962

burn their passes. In breaking up the meeting the police gunned down 69 and wounded 180. In Langa township, Cape Town, baton charges, arson and stone-throwing took over. Thirty thousand Africans marched to Parliament on March 31, led by Philip Kgosana, a university student, on behalf of the ANC.

The country was by this time in the grip of a state of emergency following closely on the Sharpeville massacre. Several protesters were arrested — ANC and PAC members alike — Mandela among them. Both organisations were banned.

Mandela's political career flourished and attained full maturity in the fifties: an era for the politics of accommodation. He was eased out of a near-exclusive passionate nationalism by his constant contact with Indian, "Coloured" and white political movements and individuals. Throughout the decade of the '50s the ANC was continually at pains to allay

◀◆▶ 1965. With their father imprisoned on Robben Island, his daughters Zeni and Zindzi were legally too young to be visitors at a prison. Later they were sent to school in Swaziland, a doubtless difficult and lonely decision for their mother, who did not want them to receive their schooling in racist South Africa.

Photographed in 1969, the late Robert Sobukwe founded the Pan Africanist Congress in March 1959, after becoming disenchanted with the ANC. The PAC organised their own anti-pass law campaign, pre-empting that of the ANC, in 1960, and Sobukwe went on record insisting that the campaign should be completely non-violent. The result was Sharpeville.

Winnie's face says it all — the first letter from her husband on Robben Island.

the fear among whites that they would be driven into the sea in the end. But at every turn the State machine rolled on relentlessly up and down the streets, grinding down those who stood in its way, releasing its bullets on those who tried to run for it.

Mandela had said in the Treason Trial:

There are two streams of African nationalism. One centres round Marcus Garvey's slogan "Africa for the Africans". It is based on the "quite Africa" slogan and on the cry "Hurl the White man into the sea". This brand of African nationalism is extreme and ultra-revolutionary. There is another stream of African nationalism, Africanism, which the Congress Youth League professes. We of the Youth League take account of the concrete situation in South Africa and realize that the different racial groups have come to stay, but we insist that a condition for inter-racial peace and progress is the abandonment of White domination and such a change in the basic structure of South African society that those relations which breed exploitation and human misery will disappear. Therefore our goal is the winning of national freedom for the African people and the inauguration of a peoples' free society

"IT WAS PRECISELY BECAUSE THE SOIL OF SOUTH AFRICA IS ALREADY DRENCHED WITH THE BLOOD OF INNOCENT AFRICANS THAT WE FELT IT OUR DUTY TO MAKE PREPARATIONS AS A LONG-TERM UNDERTAKING TO USE FORCE IN ORDER TO DEFEND OURSELVES WITH FORCE. IF WAS INEVITABLE, WE WANTED THE FIGHT TO BE CONDUCTED ON TERMS MOST FAVOURABLE TO OUR PEOPLE"
MANDELA   — RIVONIA TRIAL, APRIL 1964

where racial oppression and persecution will be outlawed.

History was to catapult Nelson Mandela into the phase of armed struggle. He and other ANC members went underground. They formed Umkonto we Sizwe (Spear of the Nation). Independent of the ANC, sabotage was its method, but ostensibly against installations rather than human life. Mandela directed several regional commands of Umkonto. June 16 experienced the first explosion, in Durban. Johannesburg followed, then Cape Town.

In 1962 Mandela sneaked out of the country to attend a conference in Addis Ababa, Ethiopia, Emperor Selassie being host. After his return, and 17 months since he went

◄■ Police were concerned at the presence of this photographer when Winnie Mandela was questioned at Park Station in 1964. In the same year she herself laid a charge of assault against the police.

underground, Mandela was arrested. He was sentenced to five years for incitement to strike and leaving the country illegally on November 7.

During 1963 some high-ranking officers of the Congress Alliance were trapped in a house in Rivonia suburb, Johannesburg. On October 9 Mandela, Walter Sisulu, Govan Mbeki, Ahmed Kathrada, Rusty Bernstein, Dennis Goldberg, James Kanlo, Andrew Mlangeni, Elias Matsoaledi and Raymond Mhlaba were put on trial on charges of sabotage and attempting

the violent overthrow of the Government.

In June of 1964 Mandela and the other accused, except for Bernstein (released) and Goldberg (imprisoned in Pretoria), were sentenced to life imprisonment. They were sent to Robben Island.

Who is this man, Nelson Rolihlahla Mandela, the dignity of whose silence transcends the vociferous pettiness of his white jailers in positions of ultimate power, the only ones who can quote him? Release Mandela? No. Release him? No, not just yet ... And so on. The ironies and contradictions, innuendos and rumours surrounding the last days of Mandela's arduous prison life are legion.

Black people who are 35 years of age today (born 1955) will have been only 5 in 1960. The 45-year-olds (born 1945) will have been 15 in 1960, just becoming politically conscious. An educated guess tells us that the most politically active blacks today fall between the ages of 25 and 35. They will not have been in a position to know Nelson Mandela.

But here is a man who has become at once the symbol of a people in chains, the agony of the sacrifice and the sustained

Mrs Martha Matlhaku, a family friend and Winnie Mandela, outside the Mandelas' Orlando West home.

Winnie Mandela at home after 13 months in detention.

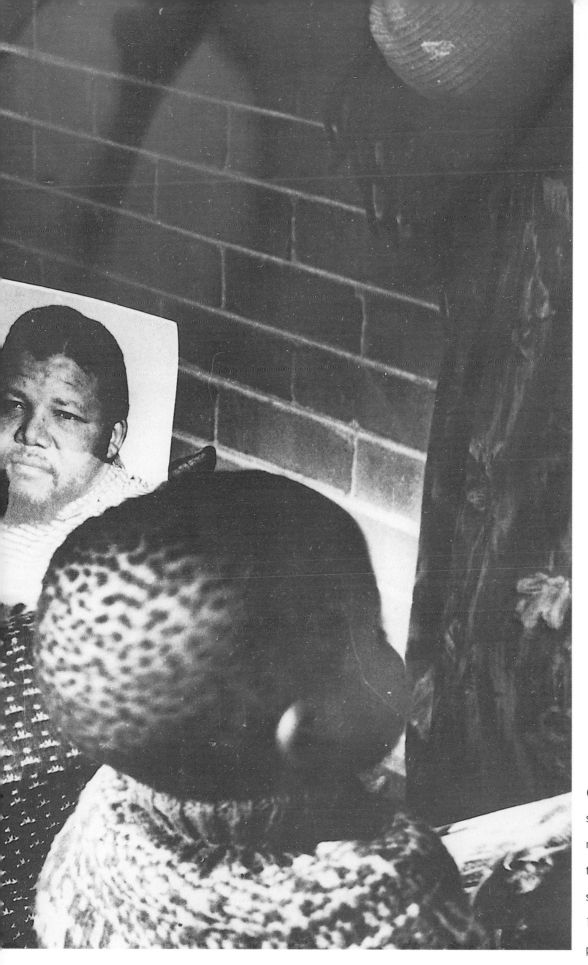

◄ The father they grew up seldom seeing. Nelson Mandela's mother, Nosekeni (Fanny) Mandela, talks to her grandchildren about her son. She died of a heart attack in 1968. The authorities refused Winnie permission to attend the burial.

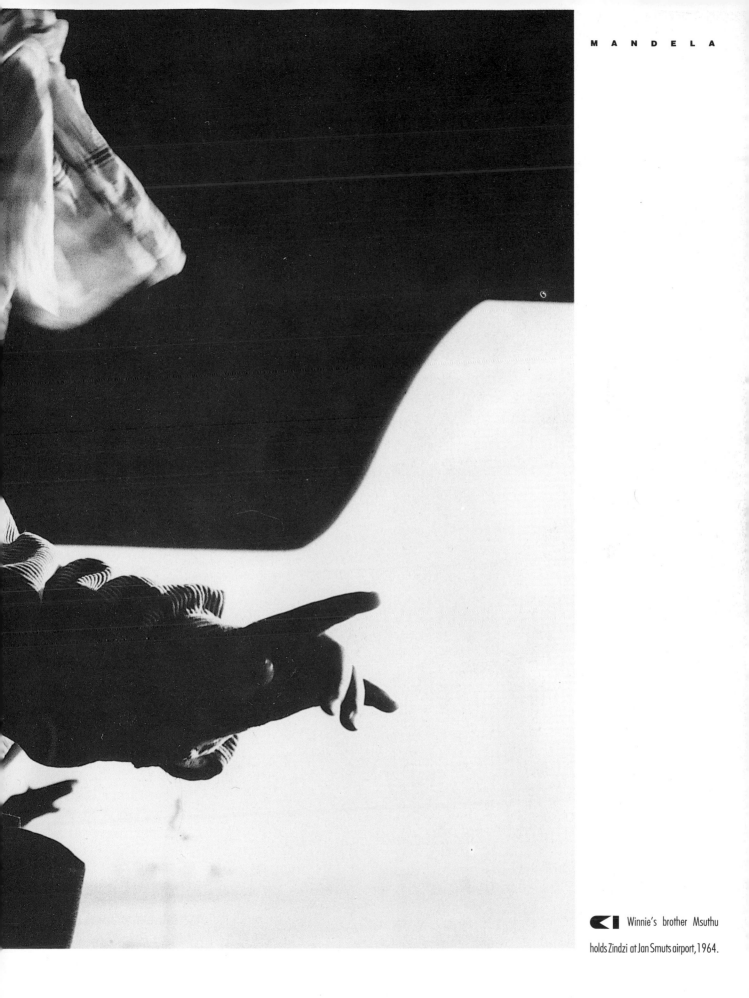

Winnie's brother Msuthu holds Zindzi at Jan Smuts airport, 1964.

"... IT IS THIS GOVERNMENT, ITS ADMINISTRATION OF THE LAW, WHICH BRINGS THE LAW INTO SUCH CONTEMPT AND DISREPUTE THAT ONE IS NO LONGER CONCERNED IN THIS COUNTRY TO STAY WITHIN THE LETTER OF THE LAW ... I DO NOT BELIEVE THAT THIS COURT IN INFLICTING PENALTIES ON ME FOR THE CRIMES FOR WHICH I AM CONVICTED SHOULD BE MOVED BY THE BELIEF THAT PENALTIES DETER MEN FROM THE COURSE THAT THEY BELIEVE IS RIGHT ... NOR WILL THEY DETER MY PEOPLE OR THE COLLEAGUES WITH WHOM I HAVE WORKED BEFORE."

M A N D E L A   — PRETORIA COURT ADDRESS, NOVEMBER 1962

◀▶ Zeni Mandela, at Jan Smuts Airport.

◀▮ Winnie and her children Zeni (5) and Zindzi (3) pictured at Johannesburg airport. Winnie was going to Robben Island to visit her husband.

inexorable energy of the people to survive their shackles.

In the last ten years at least Mandela and other political prisoners have been the source of a mounting crisis of conscience, both among those who are guilty of tyranny and among its victims, but for different reasons.

From the silence of the prison cell, prison farm, broken only by the clanging of doors and echoes of police torture, or by birdsong and scraping of crickets and cicadas, Mandela has endeared himself to the oppressed and to the liberal conscience of others.

The saga goes back 72 years to the birth of the boy Nelson Rolihlahla in Qunu, Transkei. A descendant from the lefthand (junior) side of King Ngubengcuka's household, himself tracing his lineage to Dalindyebo, Nelson went to a Christian school in the centre of Tembuland. Fort Hare College in Alice followed, where he read for the B A degree.

Under the tutelage of his foster-parent, Mandela began to appreciate African anthropology in practice, regional history and government, the sense of community and sanctity of the extended family. He got to learn that everyone who is a senior is your father, or mother or elder sister or elder brother.

Fort Hare expelled Mandela for having participated in a campus strike. Most of his

Zindzi being comforted as her mother prepares to board the plane.

subsequent education was acquired by sheer self-application, sustained by insatiable curiosity.

His elders enriched him with real-life anecdotes of the dispersion of tribes and clans resulting from internal wars where these groupings had once lived together in harmony. Intrusion by European colonists, he got to learn, had set tribe against tribe.

Nineteen forty-one: Nelson Mandela arrives in Johannesburg. The year marks the beginning of his association with Walter Sisulu, fellow-trialist and fellow-prisoner, following the Rivonia betrayal and police raid. His political family extended to include Oliver

Tambo, later his law-firm **49**

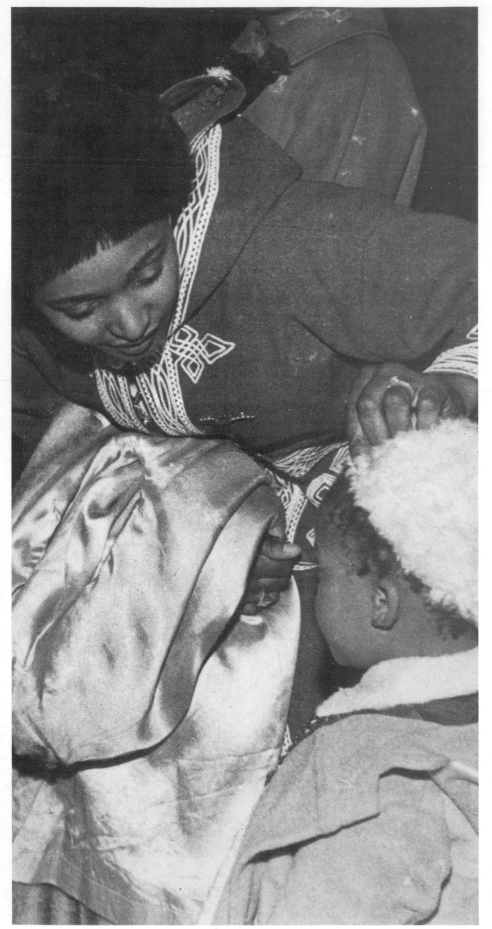

"WE WHO FORMED UMKONTO WERE ALL MEMBERS OF THE AFRICAN NATIONAL CONGRESS, AND HAD BEHIND US THE ANC TRADITION OF NON-VIOLENCE AND NEGOTIATION AS A MEANS OF SOLVING POLITICAL DISPUTES. WE BELIEVE THAT SOUTH AFRICA BELONGS TO ALL PEOPLE WHO LIVE IN IT, AND NOT TO ONE GROUP, BE IT BLACK OR WHITE. WE DID NOT WANT AN INTERRACIAL WAR AND TRIED TO AVOID IT TO THE LAST MINUTE."

M A N D E L A — RIVONIA TRIAL, OCTOBER 9, 1963 JUNE 1964.

◀◼ A final farewell to her children before boarding the flight to Robben Island.

◼▶ In August 1964 Winnie Mandela and Albertina Sisulu were allowed a visit to Robben Island. However, as banned persons, they were not permitted to travel together. Here, her eldest daughter, Zeni, weeps as her mother boards the plane.

Godfrey Pitje, who established a branch of the ANC Youth League at the University of Fort Hare in 1949. He later became the Youth League's president.

Winnie Mandela, the student. Pictured here in 1965 on her way to college. In this year she was dismissed from her job at Child Welfare.

partner, who skipped the country soon after Sharpeville (1960), becoming president of the African National Congress in exile. African nationalist Anton Lembede (died 1947) and A P Mda (now in exile in Lesotho) were other fellow-activists.

Mandela's legal studies at the University of the Witwatersrand brought him into contact with other law students who were to influence his political thinking profoundly, people such as Ismail Meer, and through him politicans such as Yusuf Cachalia and Dr Y Dadoo. His political ideas were developing and looking for a focus between

Zeni Mandela at school in Swaziland in 1971.

Steve Biko at the South African Students Organisation conference at Hammanskraal in 1972. Biko was the founder of the Black Consciousness Movement. He was later to be tortured at the hands of the South African Police and died of head injuries in September 1977 as a result. In the same year, in the aftermath of the 1976 Soweto riots, 17 organisations and two newspapers were banned by the South African Government, Minister of Justice, Jimmy Kruger, claiming that all of them supported black consciousness. It was Kruger who made the remark in Parliament when questioned about Biko's death: "I am not glad and I am not sorry about Mr Biko ... He leaves me cold."

white and Indian liberals and Marxists, like Ruth First (a Marxist, killed by a parcel bomb in Mozambique), her husband Joe Slovo (a Marxist, now on the ANC Executive), Bram Fischer (a Marxist, who died serving life on Robben Island), J B Marks and Moses Kotane (the latter two Marxists died in exile).

The ANC was beginning to evolve a militant rhetoric towards the end of the forties, as distinct from the protests intended to push for minimum power-sharing and the pleading tone and style of leadership since 1912. Men like Dr A B Xuma, more still his predecessors, were looked upon as "the old guard" by the younger nationalists. Even Chief Albert Lutuli, who became president of the ANC in 1952, was soon overtaken by an abrasive militancy developing to

"THE IDEOLOGICAL CREED OF THE ANC IS AND ALWAYS HAS BEEN, THE CREED OF AFRICAN NATIONALISM. IT IS NOT THE CONCEPT OF AFRICAN NATIONALISM EXPRESSED IN THE CRY 'DRIVE THE WHITE MAN INTO THE SEA'. THE AFRICAN NATIONALISM FOR WHICH THE ANC STANDS IS THE CONCEPT OF FREEDOM AND FULFILMENT FOR THE AFRICAN PEOPLE IN THEIR OWN LAND."

MANDELA   — RIVONIA TRIAL, APRIL 1964

A picture which poignantly illustrates the power of the Pass Laws. This man's house burnt down, leaving him destitute. He managed to salvage only his most precious possession — his identification document. The Pass Laws were abolished in April 1986.

a peak in the movement.

Nelson Mandela's role in the formation of the ANC Youth League in 1947, to which he was elected secretary, was crucial. The Youth League wrenched leadership of the ANC from Xuma and his Executive. To Lembede and Mda's slogan "Africa for the Africans" Mandela was to object as an extreme brand of nationalism.

The arrival of the Youth League on the African political landscape was even more crucial. Since its founding year, 1912, the South African Native National Congress had been led by men and women of learning and high social standing: at least three clerics, one medical doctor, a lawyer, two teachers. The presidents-general were, in chronological order: Rev John L Dube, S M Makgatho, Rev Z R Mahabane, J T Gumede, Dr Pixley Ka I Seme (the founder and lawyer), Dr A B Xuma (the last before the Youth League captured the leadership and appointed Dr J S Moroka, a medico and someone less than a dark horse).

"GREAT CARE WAS TAKEN TO KEEP THE ACTIVITIES OF THE TWO ORGANISATIONS IN SOUTH AFRICA DISTINCT. THE ANC REMAINED A MASS POLITICAL BODY OF AFRICANS ONLY CARRYING ON THE TYPE OF POLITICAL WORK THEY HAD CONDUCTED PRIOR TO 1961. UMKONTO REMAINED A SMALL ORGANISATION RECRUITING ITS MEMBERS FROM DIFFERENT RACES AND ORGANISATIONS AND TRYING TO ACHIEVE ITS OWN PARTICULAR OBJECT."
M A N D E L A   — RIVONIA TRIAL, APRIL 1964

Nelson's second son by his first wife Eveline — Makgatho Mandela.

56

◄▌ The 1970s was one of the most turbulent periods in South African resistance politics.

"HOW MANY MORE SHARPEVILLES WOULD THERE BE IN THE HISTORY OF OUR COUNTRY? AND HOW MANY MORE SHARPEVILLES COULD THE COUNTRY STAND WITHOUT VIOLENCE AND TERROR BECOMING THE ORDER OF THE DAY? EXPERIENCE CONVINCED US THAT REBELLION WOULD OFFER THE GOVERNMENT LIMITLESS OPPORTUNITIES FOR THE INDISCRIMINATE SLAUGHTER OF OUR PEOPLE."

MANDELA   — RIVONIA TRIAL, APRIL 1964

The national secretaries were, in order of service time: Sol T Plaatje, the first African investigative reporter in South Africa and famous author of *Native Life in South Africa* (1916) about the ravages of the Land Act of 1913; R V Selope Thema; E Mochochoko; T D Mweli Skota; Halley Plaatje; Rev Elijah Mdolombo, Rev James Calata, the last one before the Youth League leadership appointed Walter Sisulu.

Just before Union in 1910, three editors of African newspapers had spearheaded a meeting of African associations convened to consider the imminent cession of power by Britain to South African whites to rule the blacks. They were also alarmed at the exclusion by the Union Constitution of all persons not of European descent from Parliament.

These cultural leaders were Rev Walter Rubusana, John Tengo Jabavu (both of eastern Cape) and Rev John

◀◥ Nelson Mandela's dog — Kruschev. He was known as a formidable watchdog, guarding the family home while Mandela was in prison.

◀◢ A funeral at Avalon Cemetery in 1976. Twenty-one people had died in the townships already. Six hundred were to die in the end. In this year, Winnie Mandela was elected to the Black Parents Committee. She was detained once again and subsequently banned.

L Dube of Natal. Eventually Rubusana, Jabavu and former Prime Minister of the Cape, W P Schreiner were chosen to form a delegation to England to plead for the renunciation of the colour bar in the Constitution. They failed.

On his return from studies in the United States and England, Pixley Ka I Seme's sensibilities were outraged by the treatment of Africans by whites in the Transvaal. He assembled two other African lawyers to share with them the burning desire to see ethnic unity among Africans. To institutionalise their ideas, Seme proposed a conference to be held in Bloemfontein. January 8, 1912 thus marked the birth of the South African Native National Congress, mainly as a response to the gross and shameless betrayal of the African people in South Africa by Great Britain.

Chiefs and commoners came from as far afield as present-day Lesotho, Botswana and Swaziland. "Nkosi Sikelel'i-Afrika" was informally inducted as the African national an-

"IF THE GOVERNMENT OF THE STATE SAYS, 'WE HAVE THREE REPRESENTATIVES FOR YOU IN THE HOUSE OF ASSEMBLY, WE NOW WANT YOU TO HAVE 9, 10 OR 20' — I WOULD NOT ACCEPT THAT, BECAUSE IT IS NOT WHAT I DESIRE. I WANT THE VOTE TO BE EXTENDED TO ME. I DON'T WANT ANYBODY TO REPRESENT ME."

M A N D E L A   — TREASON TRIAL TESTIMONY, MARCH - OCTOBER 1960.

them at the convention.

Seme's motion to elect John L Dube first national president was carried. Dube was an American-trained educationalist, author and founder of Ohlange Institute in Natal, which was inspired by Booker T Washington's Tuskegee Institute in the American South as a trades school. Dube had also founded Natal's first African newspaper, *Ilanga lase Natal*.

When the notorious 1913 Land Act entered the pages of the Statute Book the Native National Congress was but an infant. But those who were at the helm of its affairs were imbued with a seriousness of purpose. The Land Act scheduled about seven and a half per cent of the country's land to be occupied by Africans. These men tried to counter the ever-increasing laws of the country in the best way they knew how: a letter or telegram of protest or deputation of the most articulate leaders, to this cabinet minister and that to place on record the indignation of the masses they represented.

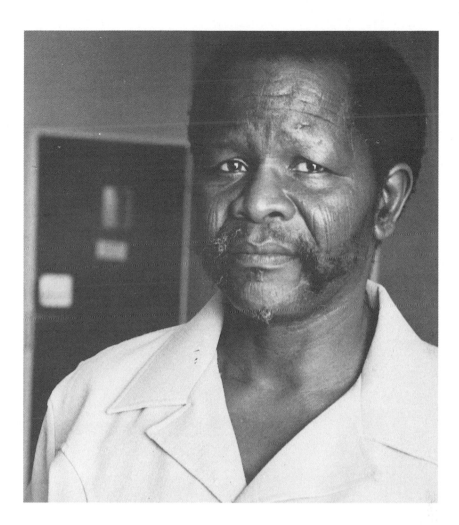

Oliver Tambo photographed in Botswana in the 1970s.

Winnie's elder sister, Niki, with her husband, Gil Xaba, and children.

By the beginning of the Youth League era the African National Congress, as the Native Congress came to be called, had witnessed the passing of one racist law after another, the Land Act (1913) following close on the introduction of the Labour Act (1911), Native Administration Act (1921), the colour bar laws on the mines. It had experienced industrial strikes, the short-lived power of the Industrial Commercial Union (ICU), led by Malawian Clements Kadalie and A G W Cham-

pion of Natal. The sequel to the Land Act of 1913 came in the form of the Land and Trust Acts of 1936. Both these deprived true Africans of their land and expelled them in droves from ancestral ground.

The Trust and Land Acts of 1936 promised to increase land for African occupation to thirteen point seven per cent: whites would release land for purchase by the government to be held in trust for African communities. In 1972 this percentage had not yet been reached. Nor could Africans buy land in the urban areas except in a miserably few

65

 Kaizer Matanzima, a cousin of Nelson Mandela, visits Winnie in Soweto. Winnie, pictured on the extreme left, is wearing traditional clothing as a mark of respect.

Photographer Alf Kumalo and Muhammed Ali. Himself a keen amateur boxer in his youth, Nelson Mandela had a copy of this photograph in his prison cell.

Winnie Mandela and her father Columbus Madikizela.

freehold ghettos. At the same time landlessness in the rural areas was forcing migrations into urban locations. This is how ghettos came into existence.

The land and trust laws had the effect of pushing African organisations towards an attempt at unity. Thus was born the All-African Convention (AAC) in the middle of 1935, a new superbody consisting of a wide range of African interest groups, including the Communist Party and the once-active members of the ICU. The paramount item on the agenda at this Bloemfontein convention was the Native Trust and Land Bills. They were naturally rejected outright. A whole range of other legislation and proclamations came under bitter criticism as well.

 Reverend Simon Nkoane being arrested after a march in 1980.

A Cape Town delegate urged that the AAC "lay the foundation for a national liberation movement to fight against all the repressive laws of South Africa". The Convention happened at a time when there were dissensions within the ANC ranks which sapped its energy, especially during J T Gumede's presidency.

For all these sentiments of disapproval against the laws, the AAC's language was as mild as the ANC had always been. In the ANC's "Programme of Action" it expressed "profound disappointment with the White parliament". All appropriate avenues of action were to be explored by the Executive Committee with the organisation's affiliates towards the achievement of common citizenship rights for all. The AAC remained vague about the precise measures it intended to take against the White parliament.

The prominent leaders of the AAC were Professor D D T Jabavu of Fort Hare College, Dr John Dube, Rev Z R Mahabane, Dr A B Xuma, Dr J S Moroka, J B Marks and the

Winnie and Nelson's daughter Zeni married Prince Dhlamini of Swaziland. Zaziwe, their first child, was christened in the Cathedral in Bloemfontein so that Winnie could attend the ceremony. Winnie had been banished to Brandfort on 16 May 1977 for five years. Two days before the expiry date of her banishment, she was informed that the order had been extended for another five years.

◄ Troops in a Western Cape
coloured township. A show of strength
while looking for petrol bombs.

Communist Party's J B Bohara and Edwin Mofutsanyana, the ICU's Kadalie. Several people straddled both the ANC and AAC in their membership.

The ANC and the AAC arrived at the former's Silver Jubilee in 1937 — the 25th year — with a mixture of renewed apprehension and hope. The Native Legislation Act of 1936 prescribed elections of "Native representatives" (white) to speak for Africans in parliament.

World War 2 raged on in the outside world. Neither the ANC nor the AAC expressed any policy towards the enlisting of blacks to inferior auxiliary service in the war. Matters stayed very much at the level of debate rather than active militancy.

The year 1946 witnessed three historic events: Gandhi's spirit of passive resistance caught the imagination of the Indian community. Second, the biggest African industrial strike (on the mines) shook the country. J B Marks took the responsibility of managing the strike. It roped in 70 000 mine workers, who downed tools over pay and the colour bar that excluded "pass-carrying natives" from all the technical jobs.

Third, the Natives Representatives Council died. There was no love lost between the Africans and the white authorities who had been created ostensibly to train "Natives" in democratic procedures concerned with parliamentary debates. Ironically the members of the elected NRC were men of substantial calibre who had entered the Council in order to break it by demanding what the Government considered impossible, by giving the debates an element of high political seriousness. In 1947 the Government killed the Council. The members had made their point.

In 1939 Rev J A Calata, then president of the Cape Congress, stated in an address to his provincial branch, "The Congress (ANC) was not established in order to fight against the Government, but in order to co-operate with it as well as other European organisations which require assistance. But that does not mean that the Congress is in any way under the influence of the Government or any organisation."

This is the stage that Nelson Mandela entered to perform his part in the Youth League in 1943-44.

In 1943, at 25 and a year after he had completed the final year of the BA degree by correspondence, he entered the University of the Witwatersrand to study law.

The war years saw the beginning of a ferment of political ideas among the younger Africans, especially students. One theatre was the Johannesburg-Pretoria area, the others Fort Hare College and teacher-training institutions such as Adams College (Natal), Lovedale (Cape) and Healdtown (Cape). These areas became the breeding grounds of the ANC Youth League.

Prominent names were Oliver Tambo and Congress Mbata, both teachers; Anton Lembede, a brilliant and distinguished young lawyer and later partner of Ka I Seme in Johannesburg; A P Mda, teacher and then lawyer; Peter Raboroko of the Provincial Students Association and ex-Fort Hare student; Nelson Mandela, Walter Sisulu, an estate agent; William Nkomo (former Fort Hare student and later medical doctor); Jordan

 Emotions ran high at political meetings. Here a man gives vent to his feelings.

Ngubane, journalist. All met to discuss the concept of the Youth League as a wing of the ANC.

They delegated some from among themselves to go and speak with Dr Alfred B Xuma, then national president.

When the group told him about the Youth League as diplomatically as they knew how, the president-general warned them not to make enemies among the rank-and-file. Xuma was not one for radical politics, street or stadium demonstrations. They had to make him see the League as a pressure group within the ANC, as an agent for "rousing popular political consciousness".

Lembede and Mda, particularly the former, were the soul of the Youth League, its driving force. They saw in it the symbol of Africanism, a custodian of traditional African values, thought and belief. They wanted to see it stand for self-reliance of the African, for nationalism that said Africa for the Africans. In 1944 the League presented Xuma with its manifesto. This document represented the League as "the personification and symbol of popular aspirations and ideals", a means of "combating" moral disintegration among Africans". Later, the constitution spoke of "educational, moral and cultural advancement". The attack on the ANC's policy and approach to oppression was unequivocal. It ruffled Xuma's dignity!

The "Basic Policy" published in 1948 referred to the 1944 event as an "historic turning point", when African nationalism became the League's creed: a creed that could "give the Black masses the self-confidence and dynamism to make a successful struggle".

Reflecting especially Lembede's thinking, the Youth League's African-ism was equivalent to African nationalism.

When the 1949 Programme of Action was tabled and adopted by the ANC the resolutions committee included A P Mda, Moses Kotane, Z K Matthews and others. The Executive Committee of the League were Mda, Mandela, Sisulu, Tambo, David Bopape and J Njongwe.

Robert Sobukwe, chairman of the Students Representative Council at Fort Hare, became one of the founders of the League's college branch in 1948, together with Godfrey Pitje. As a sign of the times, Sobukwe continually invoked Africa when he gave a graduation address at the college on October 21, 1949: "the liberation of Africa within our lifetime", "Remember Africa!", "Carry with you into the world the vision of a new Africa, an Africa reborn … an Africa recreated, young Africa!"

The Programme of Action proposed that a council of action should plan and prepare for a boycott of "all differential political institutions" and work for their abolition. The weapons were to be immediate and active boycott, strike, civil disobedience, non-cooperation, a national stoppage of work for one day by way of protest. It provided for African economic, educational and cultural advancement, similar to the contents of the ANC's 1919 constitution.

Although the passionate intensity of a Lembede was lacking in the Programme (he died in 1947), it contained an emphasis on self-determination. The spirit of the Programme was to signal a new trust in ANC politics: direct action in the place of conventional protest through delegations and telegrams and other forms of correspondence addressed to white officials.

On June 16, 1948 I B Tabata, one of the foremost figures of the All-

◄❚ More than twenty years after Mandela's life sentence to imprisonment, the eighties was a decade of continuing protest, unrest and Government retaliation. Here, out of the way of possible police action, activists line the crest of a mine dump at KwaThema township near Springs in the Transvaal during a mass funeral.

Black education has continued to be a major cause of dissatisfaction to the majority of South Africans. It precipitated the 1976 Soweto riots. It caused upheaval and boycotts in the country's townships throughout the eighties. This picture, taken at a Grasmere primary school, shows an overcrowded classroom.

African Convention, wrote a letter to Mandela. He analysed the interests that create an organisation and promote it. The ANC was "rooted in the past", he wrote, "whereas the League is the product of modern conditions, with a modern outlook". If the League pursued its goals to the final realisation, Tabata continued, "it would land itself outside the fold of the Congress".

Tabata further confirmed in the letter the historical circumstances that led to the formation of the AAC. "The fundamental idea at the time was *unity* ... to eliminate all rivalry between the organizations." Each leader was to "bring his followers, to this body and ... together with ... other organizations was to form a single leadership with a common purpose". The letter expressed the sentiment that 1935-36 was "the highest point of development in organization affecting the African people".

Tabata attacked ANC leaders such as John L Dube, Xuma, Selope Thema for being stooges who were helping the Government's repressive laws to succeed. "As members of the Youth League you speak the language of the modern intellectual — progressive, independent, rejecting inferiority. But as members of the African National Congress your language is the very negation of all these things. You accept the theory of inferiority and trusteeship... eg segregated institutions like the Native Representative Council, Advisory Boards etc."

The year the Youth League was established (1943) also saw the rise of the Non-European Unity Movement (NEUM). The Coloured Affairs Department had been established by the Government after the style of the then Native Affairs Department. The "Coloured" people in the Western Cape mounted a boycott of the department. The Western Province AAC took up the cause of the "Coloureds" in order to

Outside Regina Mundi, Soweto, the church where major commemorations and services have taken place over the years of political unrest, protesting youths take to the streets on the sixth anniversary of the Soweto Uprising.

BDX470B

spire them to identify with the Africans and Indians.

The AAC and the Anti-CAD (body boycotting Coloured Affairs) met on December 17, 943 to adopt a "Draft Declaration of Unity" and a "10-Point Programme". The Non-European Unity Movement was provisionally launched. The Programme purported to be a "principled" basis for unity. NEUM became a federal body containing the AAC which was itself made up f the Cape African Teachers' Association, the Teachers' League of South Africa (for Coloureds") and other organisations.

Between 1944 and 1947 the NEUM tried in vain to win Dr Xuma over to its drive for unity.

Tabata's no-nonsense letter to Mandela preceded the last desperate attempt at unity etween the two major organisations (at the time), with the AAC being predominantly en- renched in the Cape Province. The meeting took place on October 3, 1948, the year the Afrikaner Nationalist Party wrenched Government from Jan Smuts' United Party. The new rganisation would be called the All-African National Congress.

In 1949, at a conference of the ANC and AAC, the latter pushed for the adoption of its 0-Point Programme. The ANC resisted. After a 17-hour meeting of the executive commit- ees of the two organisations, the ANC's Moses Kotane decided that there could be no

Countless people were arrested and detained in the eighties. Here, a detainee makes a desperate (but unsuccessful) bid to escape.

◀ The funeral of victims of an SADF raid across the South African border takes place in Lesotho in 1983. This was the year in which the United Democratic Front was launched with 575 affiliated organisations.

agreement as long as Tabata and the two other men were leading the AAC. The sentiment was mutual. The bottom line of their perceived irreconcilable differences was whether the new body should be unitary in form with "federal features" or federal with "unitary features".

When negotiations fell through, however, the ANC accepted boycott as a weapon into its Programme of Action.

From this time forward the ANC was to take centre stage in African resistance politics, at any rate in the three provinces outside the Cape. It was propelled by a leadership rooted in the Youth League's nationalism — "the dynamic national liberatory creed of the oppressed African people", to quote from its 1948 manifesto.

By 1950 the influence of A P Mda on ANC policy in relation to its multiracial character had diminished but he continued to be the Youth League's theoretician and later that of the Pan-Africanist Congress. The remaining group of Youth Leaguers included Nelson Mandela, Oliver Tambo and Walter Sisulu. Clearly the ANC was learning to live with the activism of the other interest groups — the Indians, "Coloureds" and the Communist Party, although their respective policies did not immediately rhyme.

For one thing, the CP was pretty aggressive in pushing the case of the class struggle as against nationalism or Africanism. The Indian leadership represented mostly the interests of the merchant class and intellectuals. The ultimate effect of this co-existence

◀ The presence of troops in South African townships was a constant reality in the 1980s. Not all confrontations were aggressive, however. Here, young soldiers talk to youths in Soweto.

82

was that the nationalism that had originally fired Mandela and Tambo was no longer a one-way street. It had never, in any event, been as passionate, pristine and calculating as Lembede's and Mda's, which they equated with Africanism. The latter sentiment saw white people in South Africa as colonisers and/or settlers, along with Europeans who had penetrated Africa from the 19th century.

Still, the issues of nationalism, which twenty years later manifested itself as Black Consciousness, multi-racialism, non-racialism, democratic or majority rule, defy any classification according to the contending ideologies of today's South Africa. Most of the time the lines blur between them because of the overlap and a subjective sense of who "owns" which.

D E F I A N C E

Perhaps it was ironically a measure of how the ANC continued for a long time to live effortlessly in the shadow of the venerable old guard (from Dube to Xuma) that the Congress Alliance was inevitable. A unity was forged between the African National Congress and South African Indian Congress (and later the Coloured Peoples' Congress and the Congress of Democrats). In spite of the Youth League's invasion and conquest of the ANC, it turned out that the leadership was for some time to come going to be intellectuals who would be excessively cautious and ready to change stance instantly. Cynics at the time commented that the leaders knew, anyhow, that majority rule, meaning African, would eventually win out! They had nothing to lose ...

At the time Lembede, when he was alive, and Mda for a longer time, were the only

Another cross-border raid purportedly by the South African Defence Force, this time into Botswana. The aim was to destroy ANC bases, but at what cost?

83

political analysts and theoreticians who could take a hard-nosed look at the way things were going. But their stand became unpopular within the ANC leadership. The Pan-Africanist Congress was to be blessed with Mda, Robert Sobukwe and Peter Raboroko. The Unity Movement had outstanding Western Cape analysts, mostly members of the Teachers' League of South Africa.

The year 1952 marked the end of almost ten years of political apprenticeship for Nelson Mandela. He was appointed volunteer-in-chief for the Defiance Campaign due to begin on June 26. Dr J S Moroka had been dragged out of relative obscurity to have the mantle of President-General put on him. "We can now say unity of the non-European people — in this country has become a living reality." So declared Mandela. He and Tambo had recently opened a law office in Johannesburg as partners.

The Reef, Eastern and Western Cape Province, Orange Free State and Natal registered

Julius Nyerere, Oliver Tambo and Samora Machel, photographed in Botswana. Machel died in an aircraft crash in South Africa in 1986.

◣◥ Unrest in Evaton in the Transvaal — September 1984. This was the year that Release Mandela Committees were set up and the world began in earnest to demand his release. together some 8 000 people arrested for acts of civil disobedience. Most of them were symbols of petty apartheid. But the major pass laws, cattle-culling regulations, the Group Areas Act, Suppression of Communism Act, the Coloured Voters Act, which removed the "Coloureds" from the common voters' roll, the Bantu Authorities, Population Registration Act — all of them but the pass laws passed since 1950 — were being challenged through civil disobedience.

Of the Bantu Authorities Act Professor Z K Matthews of Fort Hare College and Congress Cape president, was to write, "It intended to delay indefinitely the development of a sense of national unity among Africans." According to the Act, a return would be attempted to the use of the same traditional authorities the Government had whittled down over a period of a century. It was restoring indirect rule for the expansion of a new colonialism.

In a letter to the Prime Minister, Moroka and Sisulu had written urging "democracy, liberty and harmony in South Africa". In reply the Secretary to the Minister had rebuked the ANC (January 19, 1952):

"You will realize ... that it is self-contradictory to claim as an inherent of the Bantu who differ in many ways from the Europeans that they should be regarded as not different, especially when it is borne in mind that these differences are permanent and not man-made ... The Government will under no circumstances entertain the idea of giving administrative or executive or legislative powers over Europeans ... to Bantu men and women ... The Government, therefore, has no intention of repealing the long-existing laws differentiating between European and Bantu."

◄▮ Winnie Mandela and Zindzi greet a relative at a funeral in 1984. These were the only opportunities when Winnie could obtain permission to leave Brandfort, the area to which she was restricted.

◄█ In September 1984 violence broke out in the Vaal Triangle.
Thirty-one people lost their lives.

Shades of the Old Guard of the ANC!

The leaders hauled before the judge on charges under the Suppression of Communism Act included Moroka, Sisulu, Mandela, J B Marks, Dr Yusuf Dadoo, Dr J L Njongwe and Joseph Matthews. They were given suspended sentences. Sisulu and Mandela were banned subsequently under the Suppression of Communism Act. They were declared statutory communists.

Mandela was elected president of the Transvaal ANC. Chief Albert Lutuli was elected President-General after Moroka's disgrace.

The turbulent fifties raged on. The Bantu Education Act of 1953 confirmed all our fears and the belief that once Afrikaner ideology had pissed on education, the stink would linger with us until *we* replaced the system. The removal of Alexandra Township edged towards a confrontation. It never happened. Attempts by the ANC to weaken the Government's

◄◥ Funerals during township unrest could be flashpoints for violence. Here, in Atteridgeville, Pretoria, police keep a wachful eye on mourners as they move towards the cemetery.

◄▷ In 1985 Winnie Mandela had to attend her sister's funeral without her husband. Nelson had been in gaol for 21 years.

resolve were blatantly impotent.

The 1950s was a decade of mass rallies. There was a strange fatalism about this freedom of organisation and assembly. It was as if suddenly our masses had found a voice. For the first time, too, there emerged a small class of professional politicians, even at the branch level. This freedom of assembly and association was too abundant to last, given a regime that had not the sense of humour even to allow the theatrics of our political style.

The ANC and its allies believed that mass rallies, whether or not they achieved material results, were a good agent of political education for the masses. Almost every major legislative event in Parliament touched off a reflex reaction. Indeed mass rallies did not fail to register on the Government. It took fright. Bannings became the order of the day. The police improved their methods of surveillance, perfected the techniques of torture. By 1955, forty-eight ANC leaders had been banned.

◥ A truck burns in a township street. Burnt out, smouldering vehicles were a not uncommon sight.

Looking back to failed campaigns in 1956, Z K Matthews observed, "Generally I think people are too campaign-minded and not enough organisation-minded." No wonder, then, that Mandela himself had become concerned after the Defiance Campaign about the self-abandon with which the ANC publicised its activities, with little regard for security. Hence the "M" Plan: the street cells that could discuss strategies in secrecy.

The All-African Convention, on the other hand, believed in less theatrical ways of politicising their followers. They condemned every mass dramatisation of protest as "adventurism", "undisciplined unity", "careerism" (the leadership). Their own methods emphasised the use of study circles for political education — before any major demonstration.

June 26 of almost each year since 1950, when it ushered a political strike or stay-at-home

◣◥ An ugly incident in downtown Johannesburg after a court case in which a 'Comrade' was sentenced to death in 1985. This year saw the formation of COSATU, with a membership of 500 000.

Delegates at the No[n] Alignment conference, 1985, in Harare

outside industrial control, came to be observed for some political protest or other. Demonstrations on June 26, 1952 gave the Defiance Campaign a kick-off. June 26 of 1953 was tame by comparison.

Sunday 28 was "a day of commemoration and dedication" by a request from Lutuli. It also served to launch in its own way the campaign against the removal of Johannesburg Western Areas. Mandela's and Sisulu's bannings of the previous year expired and were not renewed. The police busted a meeting, dispersing it by commands from the platform amid boos, jeers, hisses and singing.

Professor Matthews, the Cape President, suggested in his address to the 1953 provincial conference that a campaign be organised for a multiracial "Congress of the People". A national convention could be organised for the occasion, where all groups would be represented. "I wonder," Matthews said, "whether the time has not come for the African National Congress to consider the question of convening a National Convention. A Congress of the People, representing all the people of the country irrespective of race and colour to draw up a Freedom Charter for the democratic South Africa of the future."

Two months after Matthews' suggestion, the South African Coloured People's Organization (SACPO) and the Congress of Democrats (COD) were formed.

The Congress of the People met at Kliptown on the western fringes of Johannesburg on June 26, 1955. Chief Lutuli, national president of the ANC, was a banned person and could not attend. The Freedom Charter was adopted. It bore all

the marks of white liberalism, tempered by some measure of radical thinking.

The Charter demanded. all people shall vote and be responsible for the country's administration; equal rights for all racial and "national" groups; all apartheid laws shall be repealed; the wealth of the country shall be shared; the land shall be shared by all who work it; equality before the law and equal human rights; work and security for all; recognition of trade unions with all rights due to them; doors of learning to be open to all; houses; security and comfort for all; peace and friendship for all.

The group within the Congress that believed in African nationalism as defined by the late Lembede felt repudiated. They preferred to stand by the Programme of Action (1949). With reference to the white members of the Congress Alliance, the nationalist journal *The Africanist* of December 1955 stated bluntly, "NO WHITE MAN HAS EVER IMPRESSED US, liberal democrat or democratic liberal".

Africanists came to the fore to fill the vacuum left by the banning of several ANC leaders. Among the Youth Leaguers in the Africanist fold were Zeph Mothopeng, Peter Molotsi, Potlako Leballo (deceased), Josiah Madzunya (deceased) and Dr Peter Tsele (deceased).

Mandela Street in Brandfort, where Winnie spent many years as a restricted person. This picture was taken just after her house had been burnt down.

We do not seem to have any record of Mandela's thoughts about the imminent rupture in the relationship between the ANC leadership and the Africanists, nor about the on going attacks on the ANC for its alleged surrender of its initial nationalist fervour to the interests of the Communist Party and the COD in the Congress of the People. Nor do we have any sustained in-depth analysis of the ANC's ideological positions and change of stance from time to time.

We do have a clear record of his eloquent situational comments on the ANC's nationalism, but again, we do not seem to have any record of his thoughts about the All-African Convention.

There is some indication of his feelings at the 1959 split between ANC and PAC: "Banned and chained to the treason trial," writes Fatima Meer, Nelson's biographer and friend, "Nelson felt frustrated and hopeless ... He swore in anger. The government had made them impotent, cut them off from the people ... " Worst of all the trial left the field wide open to Africanists who were growing in strength. He saw them as small-minded and reactionary.

Another time Mandela dismissed with derision the PAC's efforts to discourage the call for the people to stay away from work as a protest on May 29, 30 and 31, 1961: "The efforts to sabotage the recent strike misfired badly ... And thousands upon thousands of students ... treated the PAC with utter contempt ... PAC has been shocked and stunned by the rebuff and they sit and lick their wounds."

Yet in his stay-at-home statement of May 1961, Mandela was sharply aware that leaflets had been distributed purporting to be the PAC's voice preventing the strike.

We do also have some statements of his own position on the question of nationalism:

"Africa for the Africans" versus "interracial peace and progress" and his preference of the latter. He would probably have called himself a pragmatist. He showed in his leadership an obvious single-track mind, and a fierce singleness of purpose that stood him in good stead.

There seemed to have been no room in his political career for moments of profound doubt and soul-searching. Some of his critics would even see him as aloof, unmindful of political groups outside what the ANC stood for, for example Unity Movement, Pan-Africanist Congress. Could it have been that Mandela did not want to make these other organisations feel that they were important enough to deserve his attention? Or could he have been afraid that his utterances should make the differences between the ANC and either of the other two appear bigger than was good for the nation?

Mandela's personal life was shaken up during 1953. He and his wife Eveline became estranged and despite Kaizer Matanzima's mediation, the rift came. He made it clear to Eveline that no attempt to save the 9-year-old marriage was worth the trouble. On moving out of their Orlando West home, Eveline took with her their three children — Makie (2), Makgatho (5) and Tembi (8). Both parents were hurting badly because the only sensible solution was unbearable. In 1955 they separated. In the same year Nelson met Winnie Madikizela, a social-work student.

The two fell in love. In 1958 they married.

The Congress of the People's convention at Kliptown, with its attendance of some 3 000 delegates, not only sent shivers through the ruling party in Government. It also set the stage for a major confrontation: the arrest of 156 persons, including Mandela, on charges of treason. They were arraigned for allegedly attempting to overthrow the Government by violent means.

A spin-off from the bottled-up anger of the people was its release through bus boycotts. Alexandra Township was the first to explode. The Reef took fire, than Pretoria, Eastern Cape and the Orange Free State.

Internal dissensions besides the Africanists' restlessness, corruption in the Transvaal Executive, the diminished popularity of the ANC due to its call for the suspension of the bus boycott all took its toll. The stay-away ordered for June 26, 1955 fizzled out.

In the same year Africanists walked out of the provincial congress. Matters had come to a head. Leballo, Raboroko, Madzunya, Mothopeng and Robert Sobukwe (leader) formed the Pan-Africanist Congress. The Africanists believed that they had the sympathy of larger masses than the mother-body.

At first it appeared as if the PAC were merely carping in their hostile rhetoric against the ANC's multiracialism. But their

Grim scene outside Khotso House, Johannesburg in 1986. The Nationalist Government declared a state of emergency and a massive crackdown on unionists and community leaders began.

Zindzi Mandela pictured at a mass rally where she read out a statement from her father. This was the first time the people had heard a statement directly from Mandela.

◄ In 1988 Nelson Mandela celebrated his 70th birthday, still an imprisoned man. In the same year Winnie Mandela's house was burnt down by unknown youths in Soweto. Mandela let it be known that he did not want anyone to be prosecuted for the action. News of Mandela's tuberculosis hit headlines around the world this year, when he was treated at Tygerberg Hospital in Cape Town.

criticism took on body and a dimension of earnestness that could ironically only have come of the Africanists' participation in the moulding of the ANC hitherto. They went ahead with the formation of the Pan-Africanist Congress. The inauguration happened in April 1959.

One of the factors that could not have failed to inspire optimism and idealism among the Pan-Africanists was the dismantling of European colonialism as of 1957 when Ghana became independent. In just half a decade hence all of Africa attained self-rule except the Portuguese territories and some of the smaller French colonies.

Ghana's first Prime Minister and later President Kwame Nkrumah uttered an impassioned plea at the All-African Conference held at Accra in December 1958, that we bolster up the African Personality on the freedom movement in the rest of the continent. I attended that conference while

▲ Winnie Mandela at her husband's 70th birthday celebration. A massive rock concert was staged in London in support of Mandela. The state-controlled South African media allowed no coverage of this event to be shown at home.

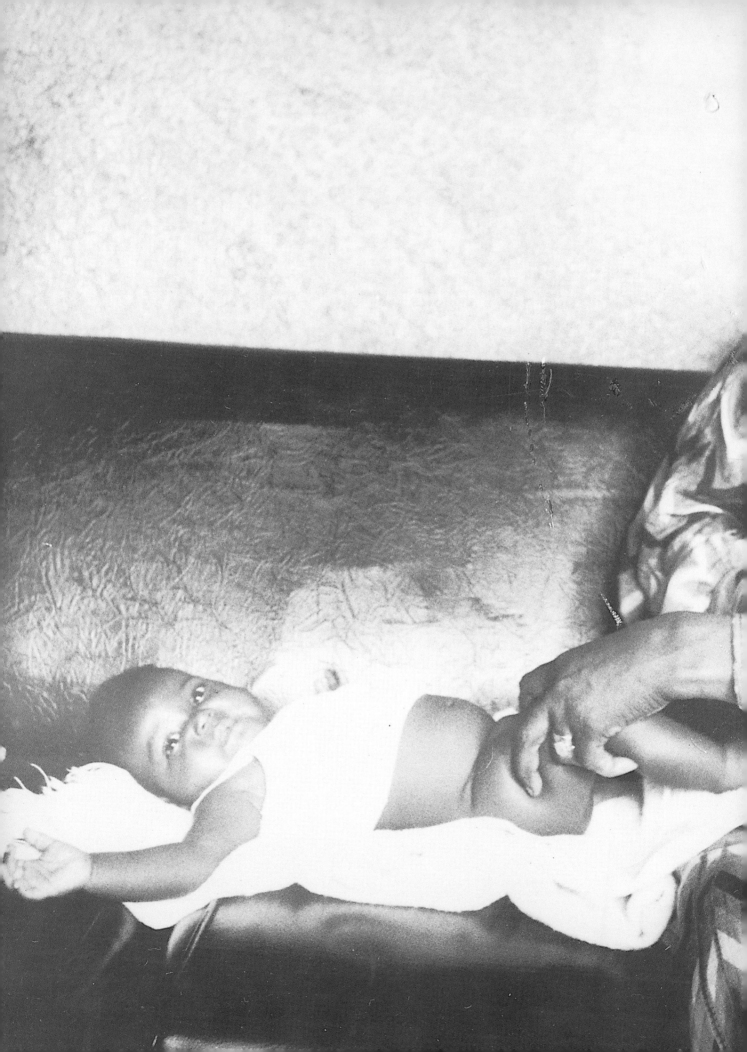

in exile, officially representing the ANC. He later urged the formation of a United States of Africa. Other historical figures in the vanguard of Pan-Africanism were Nkrumah's friends W E B DeBois, the African-American sociologist, and George Padmore, the West Indian scholar. When Pan-Africanists and ANC leaders fled into exile, they were thus moving into a changing continent, a continent in the process of becoming.

While the Treason Trial dragged on into its fourth year Sobukwe, A P Mda, Jordan Ngubane and Leballo persuaded the PAC to launch an anti-pass campaign. When March 20, 1960 dawned on this troubled land the police were waiting for thousands of campaigners on an empty field at Sharpeville. No one could have smelled evil in the air on that autumn morning. Passes were being tossed onto a bonfire. The order to disperse rode the air-waves from a bullhorn on the grandstand.

As the people sang dum-dum bullets were let loose on the crowd. The field was strewn with victims, 69 dead and scores injured. Dum-dum bullets, it was later established, explode inside the target body.

One Minister of Verwoerd's Cabinet was reported to have said, "South Africa will never be the same again!"

ANC's president Lutuli burned his pass in a public place in Pretoria days after Sharpeville as a symbolic gesture to inspire rebellion among freedom lovers. He ordered a day of mourning. Lutuli was detained, tried and released with a suspended sentence. In December 1961 he was permitted to travel to Oslo to receive the Nobel Peace Prize.

Cape Town was another major theatre of the Pan-Africanist anti-pass campaign. Philip Kgosana, a university student, led a march of thousands of demonstrators. Unfortunately the march aborted.

The ANC and the PAC were banned in April 1960 and Mandela, Sobukwe and Mothopeng were among those imprisoned. Scores were detained under the Emergency regulations.

The ANC produced and distributed from unknown quarters occasional flyers, bulletins and so on. An undated message titled "All-in African National Action Council" and signed by Mandela, secretary, appealed to students to take to the streets and demonstrate. The flyer announced that the Council had been formed at Pietermaritzburg by 1 500 delegates on 25 and 26 March 1961. It drew attention to the disaster that Bantu Education had become.

◁ Kagiso, Krugersdorp. A rare domestic picture of Winnie Mandela with her grandchild.

One of the Delmas treason trialists gets married at a ceremony attended by Archbishop Desmond Tutu and Terry Waite.

Winnie Mandela and Mr Ismail Ayob, Mandela's attorney.

Nana Mahomo and later Peter Molotsi were sent out on an external mission by PAC. So were the ANC's Tambo and Dadoo. A year later Leballo went out to Maseru, Basutoland.

The emergency lasted till August 1960. Mandela was released. On March 29, 1961 the remaining Treason Trialists were acquitted by Mr Justice Rumpf, the same judge who had nine years before acquitted Sisulu, Mandela and others from charges under the Suppression of Communism Act.

Poqo, the guerrilla wing of the PAC in the eastern Cape, issued a flyer dated March 29-31 opposing the National Action Council's directive for a stay-at-home as a protest against white domination.

R E S O R T   T O   V I O L E N C E

On May 23, 1961 Nelson Mandela wrote a letter to Sir de Villiers Graaff, chief of the United Party, requesting the whites to support the idea of a national convention:

"In one week's time, the Verwoerd Government intends to inaugurate its Republic. It is unnecessary to state that this intention has never been endorsed by the non-white majority of this country. The decision has been taken by little over half of the white community; it is opposed by every articulate group amongst the African, Coloured and Indian communities, who constitute the majority of this country.

The Government's intentions to proceed, under these circumstances, has created conditions bordering on crisis. We have been excluded from the Commonwealth, and condemned 95 to 1 at the United Nations. Our trade is being boycotted, and foreign capital is being withdrawn. The country is becoming an armed camp, the Government preparing for civil war with increasingly heavy police and military apparatus, the non-white population for a general strike and long-term non-cooperation with the Government."

Sobukwe's appeal before Sharpeville had been for "absolute non-violence". The ANC had always discouraged violence. In June 1961, after agonising over the issue, Mandela and his compatriots in hiding decided that the ANC's policy of non-violence would come to an end forthwith. Sabotage and terrorism, all-out revolution for the total overthrow of the regime, and guerrilla warfare were considered. Sabotage it was to be. The how was to be a matter of empirical assessment from time to time.

A boy runs for his life during unrest in Diepkloof, Soweto.

A self-contained fighting unit was formed to smash up industrial and state installations
and buildings. It took the name Umkonto we Sizwe (MK) — Spear of the Nation. Black and
white could become members, subject to a screening process. Umkonto was ostensibly to
be an independent body under the political direction of the Congress Alliance despite the
principles of non-violence cherished by its member organisations.

By virtue of the fact that the Communist Party intimately identified with the ANC, Marxists
such as Joe Slovo (in exile and on the Executive of the ANC), Ahmed Kathrada (released from
life imprisonment with others), Moses Kotane (deceased), J B Marks (deceased) would
naturally have gone along with the formation of Umkonto.

Although the ANC was anti-violence, it would not stop Mandela from forming Umkonto
and committing acts of sabotage, so any distinction one may attempt to make between the
two is academic. This much was understood on both sides: two sides of a coin. The ANC
would later go further and facilitate Mandela's travels and military training through its external
offices in the world's capitals.

President-General Lutuli, it is reported, was frequently consulted about these moves. He
maintained his position against violence to his dying day. But out of humility he could not
bring himself to rebuke the men of Umkonto. They were "brave, just men", he was to say after

Mandela and others had been sentenced to life in June 1964. They could not be blamed "for seeking justice by the use of violent methods; nor could they be blamed if they tried to create an organized force to ultimately establish peace and racial harmony ... They represent the highest in morality and ethics in the South African political struggle."

July 21, 1967. Lutuli was killed during a walk near his Groutville (Natal) home. The story was that he had been knocked down by a train.

Lutuli had asked for a National Convention to be jointly sponsored by the ANC and the PAC in May 1961. After several setbacks, not least of which was the dramatised rivalry between ANC and PAC and a court case in which both were indicted by the State as banned organisations, the convention was held. It was reported a great success. The high point of that conference was the dramatic appearance of Mandela. Lilian Ngoyi's presence was no less electric amidst roofshaking applause. Lilian was head of the ANC Women's League.

June 26, 1961. Nelson Mandela, as secretary of the All-in Action Council, issued a press statement. He commended the people on the successful 3-day strike. He predicted that the Nationalist Government would not survive long if the people worked harder and more systematically. He called again on the Verwoerd Government to hold a National Convention.

Mandela continued to elude the police after having gone underground in April 1961. After Umkonto was established he realised that it had to develop into an efficient war machine. The ANC sent him out to other African countries to solicit support. In 1962 he attended the Pan-African Freedom Movement for Central, East and Southern Africa in Addis Ababa. He had to find out where military training facilities existed for the MK. He also met up with Oliver Tambo.

The tour took Mandela to West, East and Central African countries, where he met such outstanding leaders as Presi-

◀◼ Nelson Mandela's first wife Eveline, cousin of Walter Sisulu, pictured in her store in the Transkei. She is the mother of Mandela's two sons Tembi and Makgatho, and his daughter Makie. Tembi was killed in a car accident in 1969.

dents Nyerere, Sekou Toure (Guinea), Léopold Sédar Senghor (Senegal), Modibo Keita (Mali), K Kaunda (present-day Zambia), and the Emperor of Ethiopia, Haile Selassie.

He returned in June 1962.

Two months later Mandela left the family for Durban to see Lutuli and others. His old friends Ismail and Fatima Meer, Dr Naicker and M R Yengwa were there to meet him. In Pietermaritzburg the police caught up with Nelson. They took him in handcuffs to Johannesburg.

He and Sisulu were indicted for incitement. In the midst of evocations, cheers and song in court that expressed the love for two heroes, the magistrate sentenced Mandela to 3 years' imprisonment for inciting the people plus 2 years for leaving the country without valid travel documents. Sisulu was hit for 6 years, but was released on bail. He disappeared underground. Albertina, Sisulu's wife, was detained for 90 days.

Mandela began his term at Pretoria Central Prison and then was carried to Robben Island. His wife Winnie could

◄ Allan Boesak, Winnie Mandela and Helen Joseph.

not see him as she was under a ban since about February 1963.

Although Winnie's Orlando West home had been open season for police raids ever since her husband went underground in 1961, this ban was the beginning of a long series of police raids. Eight months after Nelson's prison term began he was allowed his first visit.

The night of July 11, 1963, Rivonia. The story of the raid on the peri-urban estate in Rivonia sends a chill down one's spine, precisely because we've never known the details leading to that eventful cold night, which thus intensifies all the more our sense of treachery. We feel cold-blooded betrayal was in the air; that the arrest of the Congress Alliance leaders in the house was inevitable. The ancient Greek gods were laughing!

October 9, 1963. The historic trial begins in Pretoria.

The funeral of Dr James Moroka. He was president of the ANC in 1949 and during the Defiance Campaign years, succeeding Dr A B Xuma.

Winnie Mandela gives the salute at a mass funeral of victims of the Alexandra massacre.

Mandela, brought out of the Island, with nine others are in the dock. Winnie has been allowed to attend, after an initial refusal. Some of the big guns that are then brought in on political trials are there: Bram Fischer, Arthur Chaskalson, Joel Joffe. The case is named "The State versus the National High Command and others".

Accused are: the High Command and Umkonto we Sizwe: Nelson Mandela, Walter Sisulu, Dennis Goldberg, Govan Mbeki, Ahmed Kathrada, Lionel Bernstein and Raymond Mhlaba. The others: James Kantor, Elias Motsoaledi, Andrew Mlangeni, Bob Alexander Hepple. Six Africans, one Indian, four whites.

The charge: "The accused deliberately and maliciously plotted and engineered the commission of acts of violence and destruction throughout the country directed against the offices and homes of State and municipal officials, as well as against all lines and manner of communications ..."

It went on to accuse the men of planning chaos in South Africa, disorder and turmoil in which thousands of guerrilla war units would take part. MK also had honourable mention. Lilliesleaf farm in Rivonia and Travelain in Krugersdorp were alleged to have been purchased as bases for underground activities. Key State witnesses were referred to as "X" and "Z". They were members of Umkonto, which Mandela acknowledges.

Mandela's defence, like the one he presented with admirable eloquence and poise in Pretoria in November of 1962, is a remarkable narrative of tyranny. It is tyranny that is equipped with a formidable arsenal against unarmed but stubborn endurance. He portrays an oppressed people armed with nothing except a will to survive the barbarism of the State.

A history unfolds in this narrative of the changing fortunes of the ANC, its misgivings, misjudgments, naiveté, idealism, sense of realism, African humanism, Christian-inspired pacifism. With hindsight one realises that there was no way the forces of good could have won the day. Mandela must have known this. To think that white South Africa listened to this man's reasonableness with a cynicism: you tell untruths, you hang. You tell the truth, you hang anyway ... It is a cynicism dense enough to blind the sun, as we say, knowing full well that he was condemned long before he was arrested.

Guilty of sabotage. Mandela, Sisulu, Mbeki, Motsualedi, Kathrada, Mhlaba and Goldberg, Mlangeni. That day in 1964 seems but yesterday now that these men were released — in October 1989. All but Mandela.

In whatever guise the ANC and the PAC have reappeared since they were banned in 1960. The liberation front or more exactly the human spirit that informs

◀ Police and the Mandela Football Team clash at the funeral of Mrs Irene Mkwayi . Winnie Mandela is pictured on the extreme right.

progressive forces, has been marching to several drummers.

Potlako Leballo's theatrical manner laid the members of Poqo, the PAC's guerrilla wing, wide open to mass arrests in 1963. He announced from Maseru that there were PAC cells all over South Africa. They would all rise to create widespread damage to life and property where the whites were. Basutoland police clamped down on local PAC leaders while South African authorities were collecting, it was reported at the time, some 3 246 members of Poqo, which all coincided with the passing of the General Law Amendment Act in May 1963. Under this law a person could be detained for 90 days at a time, renewable each time it expired. This was for the purpose of isolating a detainee, in solitary confinement if need be, to grill him or her, torture them if that is what was required.

Sobukwe's 3-year prison sentence was due to expire on May 3, 1963. He was detained for a further period on Robben Island under a special "Sobukwe Clause". The General Law Amendment Act provided for such a clause. He was released 6 years later and confined in 1969 to Kimberley under 12-hour house arrest. Having studied economics and law in

Winnie arrives at the Victor Verster Prison in Paarl to visit her husband on his 71st birthday. Present were his son Makgatho, his wife and their son.

Family members
converge in Paarl to celebrate
Mandela's birthday.

prison, Sobukwe was articled in Kimberley. In 1975 he set up his own law office. After a protracted illness Sobukwe died. He was buried at his original home in eastern Cape.

In 1961 the African People's Democratic Union of South Africa (APDUSA) was formed as an affiliate to the Non-European Unity Movement (NEUM). I B Tabata, Cape Town's veteran activist of the All-African Convention, was one of APDUSA's pioneers and became its president. After a ban of five years, Tabata skipped the country in 1963. Now in Lusaka, Zambia, he still holds the presidency of both the Unity Movement of South Africa and APDUSA. He continues to be the theoretician of Unity Movement activism.

From 1964 to 1967 Verwoerd's Government remained the sole visible player on the stage of South African politics. There was not a challenger in sight. On September 6, 1966 Verwoerd was butchered at a Cabinet meeting by a white immigrant cleaner the Government declared insane immediately after the event. John Vorster, formerly Minister of Police, succeeded Verwoerd.

The Government had over a number of years endeavoured to tighten conditions to slow down almost to a halt the influx of Africans to the towns and cities. The Land Act of 1913, the Urban Areas law and their amendments, the influx control regulations, the reservation of skilled jobs for whites, the Bantu Administration laws and their amendments — all these and

other legislative measures constituted the ideological arsenal intended to put the blacks in their place. They had to
be taught to regard themselves as sojourners in the
whiteman's town or city merely to work and return to their
"homelands".

In order to kill African nationalism, or at least slow down
its growth and influence, Verwoerd, and after him Vorster
and P W Botha, made sure that all administrative structures
were set up to "control the natives", and entrench ethnicity.
In township residence and at school we were to belong to
a particular language / ethnic group, to know where one was
allowed to be.

By 1976, the watershed in the history of education due
to the revolution on school campuses, it became evident to
the Government that it could not enforce ethnic and/or
language divisions. That part of the Grand Design col-
lapsed, as did the attempts to make African languages the
media of instruction in school from the primary through the
Matric level.

The Nationalists succeeded to some extent in conning
some rural leaders into accepting self-rule in order to lock
Africans into enclaves where they could administer their
own underdevelopment. The Government took over what
was municipal government attached to some town or city
and operating as a "Non-European Affairs Department".
Municipal services deteriorated badly under "Administration Boards" answerable to the central department that is
supposed to look after our affairs. All local administrations
are now heavily in debt, there are long-standing rent boycotts and widespread refusal to pay for electricity and
water.

The only other actor on the stage of South African politics
came to be Mrs Winnie Mandela. But then she has always
been the victim rather than an actress who could happen to
events rather than the other way around.

In 1969 she and 21 others were held in detention for 6
months. When they were formally charged with terrorism,
loyalty between them had become frayed and they ratted on

◀ Makgatho Mandela, his son, his sister Makaziwe (Makie) and their
children photographed in July 1989.

one another. They were acquitted the following year after harrowing interrogation and torture. They had scarcely left the courthouse when Winnie was re-arrested and held another 6 months in solitary confinement. Acquittal followed yet a second trial on the same charges.

An earlier banning order expired while Winnie was in jail. It had not been renewed. Instead they hit her with another ban, this time for five years.

Police raids of the Mandela home continued almost relentlessly. In 1974 Winnie and the internationally renowned photographer, Peter Magubane, lost their appeal against a conviction of six months in jail for communicating while she was under a ban. They served the sentence.

The 5-year ban was not renewed in 1975 and she went to Durban for a welcome. They elected her onto the executive of the Federation of Black Women.

Detention orders caught up with Winnie again in July 1976, when Soweto school children were on the rampage. The police and the army killed no fewer than 500 children during the high point of the revolt of those days. The orders were withdrawn, but not before the rebellion had spread like a bushfire to Cape Town's townships and other areas of Transvaal.

Many children fled into exile, some hardly 14 years of age. Winnie was released on December 30, 1970. She was banned again and faced five years' house arrest. During such time she could not receive visitors. Lilian Ngoyi and Helen Joseph of the ANC Women's League had by then begun their long road of solitude under house arrest. Winnie had to report daily at the police station. This meant that she could not attend meetings of either the Women's Federation or the executive of the Black Parents' Association which she took part in establishing as soon as the crisis in the schools broke out.

May 16, 1977. Winnie was banished to a small Orange Free State town, Brandfort. Harassment by the police continued during her stay there.

In December 1981, Winnie was slapped with another ban for 5 years when the previous 5 years' restriction

◄■ Press conference held in Johannesburg after the release of the 'Sisulu Seven'. Winnie Mandela is seated in the row behind them, fist raised.

expired. She endeared herself, so reports went, to the people of Brandfort. From the little municipal hovel she occupied, she worked with the Brandfort women at vegetable gardening.

During the Brandfort sojourn Winnie could receive visitors, one at a time.

She was awarded an honorary doctorate in 1982 by Haverford College, Pennsylvania, USA. Her daughter Zindzi received it on her behalf.

In spite of repressive measures, the PAC and the ANC still had thousands of people loyal to them, no matter what the constraints, and to suggest that nothing was happening on the political platform is to oversimplify the social climate. It is not unusual that when a new idea or ideas surface the first shout comes from university and college campuses.

The Publications and Entertainment Acts had been passed in 1963, so the censors instituted by the Act had been sharpening their knives by the time a spate of publishing was on among university students. The first chairman of the Publications Board was ruthless. Revolutionary pamphleteering here and abroad suffered a severe blow being continually cut off from a South African audience. There was in a sense a climate of organised cultural illiteracy.

The National Union of South African Students (NUSAS), an organisation consisting of liberal-minded students, mostly from liberal homes, was the sole body articulating the aspirations of its black membership. Blacks tended to hitch their wagon to the NUSAS post. But it also meant the whites could only articulate the aspirations of the underdog from their own perceptions. Furthermore, there has always been a gross imbalance between education for whites and for blacks, qualitatively and quantitative.

This meant that there were certain imperatives in black education which were not shared by white students and their communities. Eventually the black students broke away from NUSAS after several attempts to align the aspirations of the whites with those of the blacks or vice versa.

Between 1967 and 1968, brilliant young Steve Biko emerged with a razor-sharp intellect. He stormed the citadel

◄▌ Celebrations at the welcome home rally.

that was NUSAS. He had come from the stormy eastern Cape. Under his leadership, the South African Students' Organisation (SASO) was formed. Biko was then at the University of the North. He said at the time:

"We are concerned with that curious bunch of non-conformists ... that bunch of do-gooders that goes under all sorts of names — liberals, leftists etc. These are the people who argue that they are not responsible for white racism ... These are the people who claim that they too feel the oppression just as acutely as the Blacks and therefore should be jointly involved in the Black man's struggle ... These are people who say that they have black souls wrapped up in white skins."

The concept of Black Consciousness came to define for its adherents the awareness of one's African cultural origins; of the need and desire to be self-reliant, to be proud as Africans. Pro-

◄■ "Long Live ANC!" Release of the ANC activists headed by Walter Sisulu.

125

grammes of education and cultural activity were created by SASO in several rural and urban centres.

Then the police did the unpredictable and unbelievable. They murdered Biko on September 2, 1977 while they held him in detention. Unpredictable because Biko was the opposite of integrationist although he did not in the least support ethnicity. Whatever was going to be the dominant culture in this country was going to have to be on the black people's terms. We were not going to wait for whites to determine the cultural destiny of black people. Black was by SASO's definition going to include Africans, "Coloureds" and Indians — ie all people who are not officially designated white.

The Minister of Justice, Jimmy Kruger, banned all Black Consciousness and other organisations and education programmes sponsored by SASO on October 19. Included under the ban were the Black Peoples Convention, South African Students' Movement, Black Community Programmes.

The trial of the "SASO Nine" began in Pretoria on May 2, 1976 — just the year before Steve Biko died. For three years he had been banned. Saths Cooper was one of the chief accused. The charges included endangering the maintenance of law and order; alternatively, "conspiring to transform the state by unconstitutional, revolutionary and/or violent means", creating and fostering "feelings of racial hatred, hostility and antipathy by the Blacks toward the White population group of the Republic", discouraging, hampering, deterring or preventing "foreign investment in the economy of the Republic".

Although SASO and the Black Peoples Convention were found to be not revolutionary organisations, all nine accused were sentenced to 5-6 years on Robben Island.

The significance of this phase in resistance politics is indicated in what Steve Biko wrote:

"The call for Black Consciousness is the most positive call to come from any group in the Black world for a long time. It is more than just a reactionary rejection of Whites by Blacks. The quintessence of it is the realization by Blacks that, in order to feature well in this game of power politics,

◀▌ Walter Sisulu joins in the singing of South Africa's national anthem —
N'kosi Sikele i Afrika.

they have to use the concept of group power and to build a strong foundation for this ... [It] expresses group pride and the determination by the Blacks to rise and attain the envisaged self."

Of course just before the seventies came in, African-Americans had rediscovered themselves as a result of what they perceived as Black Consciousness. They too had been through cycles of nationalism, negritude, Black Consciousness.

Black Consciousness became institutionalised in the banned organisations — BCP, BPC. In their place AZAPO was formed: Azanian Peoples' Organization. Side by side with it has been Azanian Students Movement (AZASM) and, more recently, Azanian National Youth Union (AZA-NYU). There is now also the Black Consciousness Movement (BCM) which was formed in exile.

It would not be an exaggeration to say that Black Consciousness as a state of mind is pervasive. It can be found buried in the subconscious of every person who feels oppressed because of his skin colour and race. It even manifests itself among those who would assert that Black Consciousness is a kind of racism and is therefore exclusive. Biko himself explained that it was neither racist nor undemocratic to be proud of your colour and culture, to mobilise our rural resources for self-reliance.

It gave an impetus to a great deal of writing throughout the seventies and into the eighties. An encouraging sign is the Mass Democratic Movement. Scarcely two years old, it has so far been able to assemble into itself the United Democratic Front and its affiliates, AZAPO and other Black Consciousness groups, Pan African Movement and its affiliates. This includes trade unions who are attached to UDF, Black Consciousness and Pan Africanism.

◀ Kenneth Kaunda, Alfred Nzo and Walter Sisulu at the Lusaka Conference.

It is arguable that the students' revolt which began on June 16, 1976 happened when it did because a climate of student unrest existed, occasioned over a long time by Bantu Education and campus discontent, and fuelled by Black Consciousness. Black universities have been breeding grounds for activism since 1960 when they were established. They were conceived by the Nationalists as centres of ideological control first and foremost and hardly as institutions of humanistic learning and academic freedom.

Until very recently, the universities were fenced in like prisons or fortresses. The police have always been quick to raid them, to haul out students to put them in detention. The army has for a long time been a common sight in the townships. Already the 1976 to 1978 schools revolt was but an extension of an ugly mood that had been building up both on university and school campuses for a long time.

In the year that Black Consciousness units were scattered by banning order on October 19, 1977, Vorster instructed P W Botha, then Minister of Defence, to plan for and come up with a blueprint of a tricameral parliament. There would be three chambers — for "Coloureds", Indians and whites and a joint Council of Ministers. This was meant to placate the hostile international attitude that had built up.

Even at the time when this was being discussed in Government circles, plans

◄▌ Mr Walter Sisulu meets Mr Alfred Nzo, Secretary General of the ANC, in Lusaka shortly after his release from prison. Albertina Sisulu is on the left and the man wearing an overcoat is Mr Zulu, a senior minister in the Zambian Cabinet.

were afoot among blacks to regroup as a broad liberation front. Black fury had been touched off. Thus were born the United Democratic Front and the National Forum. In August 1983 the UDF was launched under the leadership of Archie Gumede, Albertina Sisulu and Oscar Mpetha, all three veterans of the ANC-that-was.

When it became evident that the UDF was winning into its home about 500 organisations, the Government responded in typical fashion: raids on offices and detentions.

When Saths Cooper, one of the SASO-BPC Nine came out of Robben Island in 1983, he joined hands with another ex-Robben Islander, Neville Alexander, to think up a way of responding to the tricameral charade. The National Forum was the result. It met at Hammanskraal for its launching.

The National Forum participants criticised the UDF which they believed tended to perceive the struggle for freedom simply as a thrust towards "civil rights", the removal of apartheid legislation. The UDF, it was pointed out, did not see the struggle as a revolutionary effort, ie an effort to overthrow the whole regime and its capitalist system.

When the people of the Vaal Triangle began to boycott rents in 1983 the immediate cause was high rents for inferior housing and services. And yet, as so often happens in industrial labour, a single strike or boycott drags in a load of political grievances that have been rankling in the people's minds. The strike or boycott or stay-at-home no longer has a solely economic basis. People just get fed up with the whole package of things the system expects them to swallow if they try to live with other less harsh conditions. So the rent boycott was actually a way of attracting attention to bigger political issues as well.

◄█ Lusaka, January 1990. Andrew Mlangeni and the exiled leader of the South African Communist Party, Joe Slovo. Slovo is a member of the ANC executive.

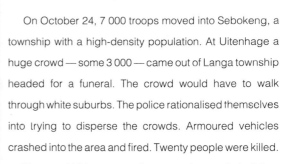

On October 24, 7 000 troops moved into Sebokeng, a township with a high-density population. At Uitenhage a huge crowd — some 3 000 — came out of Langa township headed for a funeral. The crowd would have to walk through white suburbs. The police rationalised themselves into trying to disperse the crowds. Armoured vehicles crashed into the area and fired. Twenty people were killed.

The year 1984 saw more demonstrations and a build-up of UDF morale. Shades of what Z K Matthews called "campaign-minded" in the place of "organization-minded"...

The UDF-affiliated Council of South African Trade Unions (COSATU) and the National Council of Trade Unions (NACTU) became a reality, after a long period of scattered and directionless unions. The most important hurdle both federations have still to clear is the question how far one should allow sectional ideologies to determine affiliation of a union and individual membership in a union.

P W Botha declared a state of emergency in 36 magisterial areas. In three months 5 000 people had been detained. Meetings were banned. Anonymous killings were committed. The Government suspended the emergency. In 8 months since its introduction about 8 000 people were detained. Of these 2 000 were under 16 years of age. More than 700 died in conditions of violence.

The State's Bureau of Information began launching the news. Press censorship became harder to circumvent and even more vicious than ever before. The renewal of the State of Emergency made things even tougher for activists and the press. Any news story related to violence had to be screened by the Bureau to blunt the blade of painful truths.

Till this day a newspaper may be warned that it is slanting its news in a way that creates a bias against the Government or shows the State in a bad light. Another warning may lead to the banning of a particular issue or for a longer period.

The pass laws with influx control regulations were repealed in 1986. The Bureau published its own version of

A ray of hope for South Africa. A boy bows his head in prayer after the announcement of ANC leader Nelson Mandela's impending release.

news about certain incidents of violence or unrest. It then handed over this task to the Public Relations division of the police. This happened through 1987.

Organisations had the scope of their functions limited to administration rather than human contacts in which the social or political significance comes into play. These restrictions applied to organisations such as the UDF, Detainees Parents Support Committee and AZAPO, and came into force in 1988.

For some time now a kind of civil war has been raging in Natal between UDF supporters and members of Inkatha, Chief Buthelezi's organisation. All attempts to hold conciliation or peace talks have aborted.

The Conservative Party stepped into the place of the Progressive Federal Party in 1987 as the official Opposition. The latter party later disbanded and reformed as the Democratic Party just before the 1989 'general' election.

When the eight ANC and one PAC men were released from their life sentences in October 1989, the air was charged with sheer jubilation and euphoria. The welcome home rallies which were laid on for them — for the eight in Johannesburg, for the one at Atteridgeville, Pretoria — amply demonstrated that we had come full circle in our organised politics. The optimism, the idealism of the fifties, the ecstasy of being part of a forward motion, repeated at the time of Sharpeville, and now in 1989 were back with us.

Two months later Terror Lekota, Popo Molefe, Tom Manthata and others came out of jail after four years of imprisonment. They had been arrested in 1984 when leading the rent boycott in the Vaal Triangle.

The spine-chilling disclosures of police hit squads rocked the country at the end of 1989. Among the many victims were well-known activists Mr and Mrs Mxenge (lawyers in Durban), Dr and Mrs Rebeiro of Mamelodi, Pretoria and Wits academic David Webster. Several were exiles.

Disclosures came initially from a death-row prisoner, Nofemela himself a member of a hit squad, who implicated former police captain Dirk Coetzee. Coetzee fled the coun-

◀ Elias Motsoaledi and Cyril Ramaphosa at the Lusaka Conference.

try and went into hiding. He confirmed Nofemela's disclosures and suggested that these were only the tip of the iceberg. A judicial commission of inquiry has since been appointed to investigate acts of violence "allegedly committed with political motives".

This is the world to which Nelson Mandela will be returning. In the weeks preceding the return of the eight (plus Mbeki) and in the following weeks, the questions have largely been: what deal, if any, is being worked out between Mandela and President de Klerk? And what took place at Tuynhuys, P W Botha's residence, when Mandela was invited there for tea? Who was stalling on the matter of his release?

In the first month of 1990, the news broke of Mandela's conditions for his release: the ending of the state of emergency, the scrapping of restrictions placed on 30 organisations, the unbanning of the ANC. These demands are considered in several quarters to be extraordinarily mild.

From Robben Island in 1964, to Pollsmoor Prison on the mainland, to a prison farm near Paarl — what a journey for this man, Nelson Mandela who has never been forgotten, and whose release has been fought for and awaited for so long.

 F W de Klerk, President of South Africa, announced to Parliament on February 2, 1990, that he was unbanning forthwith the African National Congress, the Pan-Africanist Congress and the South African Communist Party. Forty-two years of white nationalist rule, during which the parliament of white people has been a busy buzzing hive of legislative mischief and merry-go-round debates between so-called *verkramptes* and so-called *verligtes*. Thirty years of these during which the main resistance movements were voices from the underground.

Mr de Klerk went further: the release of all political prisoners who had not committed an "ordinary" crime for political purposes. All members of the ANC and PAC

◄❙ Andrew Mlangeni arrives home at Jan Smuts airport after the historic meeting in Lusaka.

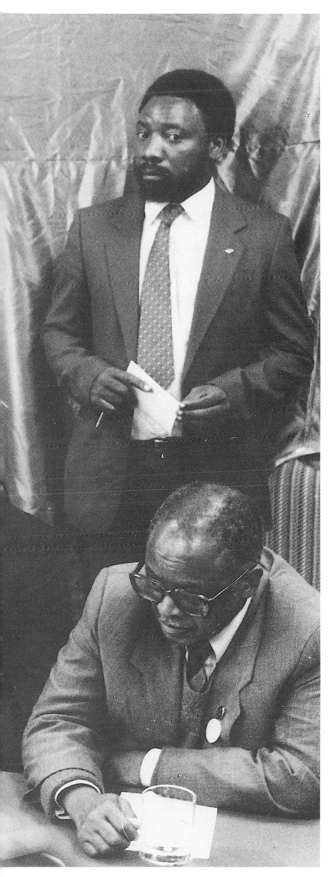

would be allowed to return on the same condition that determines the phrase "genuine" political exiles. Nelson Mandela would be relased as soon as certain security formalities had been fulfilled.

Emergency restrictions on 33 organisations were removed. The United Democratic Front, Council of South African Trade Unions, Azanian Peoples' Organisations and others would be free to operate again. Emergency regulations related to the media and education were lifted to the last item, but security measures would be protected and amended to retain efficient control on media and their visual portrayal of violence and other kinds of unrest.

People would still be detained without trial but for a reduced period of 6 months instead of an indefinite period of time as in previous cases.

In addition De Klerk suspended the death sentence until Parliament has considered certain reforms. Judges would no longer be entirely bound by the mandatory penalty for certain crimes.

The right to appeal would be automatic.

The President's reasons for lifting the ban against the three organisations were: the bigger two had moved significantly, he believed, towards "peaceful solutions". The three were no longer a threat to security. Communism, he claimed, was collapsing in Eastern Europe, so those three organisations would no longer receive financial aid from that part of Europe.

Mr de Klerk speculated that Mandela would play an important part in "constructive negotiations". The African leader, he said, had expressed a desire to do just that.

In this agenda-is-open mood, De Klerk is considered to have earned himself a clean bill of health from the Americans and the British.

Yet how many martyrs has it taken — and will yet take — to bring down political tyranny of this magnitude, of such long duration? And what of the men who called Mandela a terrorist, leader of an organisation that stood for violence? Verwoerd, Vorster, both dead, and Botha forced out of power by his party. Can President de Klerk deny that he takes equal responsibility for Cabinet decisions taken from time to time to keep Mandela and the other political lifers behind bars?

When finally the heart of white South Africa is ripped open for all to see, will its conscience yet acknowledge the irreparable damage it has inflicted on thousands of lives on this side of the colour line?

Who will atone?

◀ Delegates from the Lusaka Conference held a press conference on their return to South Africa. From left: Murphy Morobe (standing), Assistant Publicity Secretary for the United Democratic Front, Walter Sisulu, Govan Mbeki, Beyers Naude, Andrew Mlangeni, Cyril Ramaphosa (standing) and Elias Motsoaledi.

prOLOGUE

On Sunday, 11 February 1990, at approximately 4 pm, Nelson Mandela was released unconditionally after 26 years as a political prisoner, first on the notorious Robben Island, then at Pollsmoor Prison in Cape Town and finally at the Victor Verster prison near Paarl in the Cape Province.

Watched by the eyes of the world, Mandela and his wife Winnie gave the ANC salute as together they walked to freedom out of the prison gates.

 Cape Town's Grand Parade, 11 February 1990. Crowds had been gathering all day, waiting to hear Nelson Mandela's first words to the nation.

 Soccer City outside Soweto. A mass welcome home rally for Nelson Mandela drew 130 000 followers from all over South Africa. The two white men invited onto the platform were Advocates George Bizos and Arthur Chaskalson (wearing glasses), both of whom played key roles in the Treason Trial.

Nelson Mandela, Tuesday, 13 February 1990, at the rally to welcome him home.

Nelson Mandela, Walter Sisulu and Andrew Mlangeni on the platform during the welcome home rally. Tuesday, 13 February 1990.

◄■ A private word exchanged between the two veteran leaders of the ANC, Nelson Mandela and Walter Sisulu.

◄▮ Crowds wait patiently for Mandela outside his Orlando West home in Soweto. Newsmen and cameramen from networks around the world had set up their equipment here days in advance of his arrival.

▮► Nelson and Winnie Mandela together at home in Soweto.

◄▮ Winnie and Nelson Mandela with Mr and Mrs Zeph Mothopeng. Mothopeng is the leader of the Pan Africanist Congress, and was a neighbour of the Mandelas and a political comrade of longstanding.

A day with family and friends — Winnie and Nelson Mandela at home.

152

Children climb the wall of the Mandela home, hoping for a glimpse of the ANC leader.

◀▌ At home in Orlando West, Nelson Mandela greets old friends and comrades. Here Archbishop Tutu and his wife Leah arrive at the house.

◀▶ Relaxing at home, Nelson Mandela takes time to get to know his nephews and nieces. Brother-in-law Gil Xaba, husband of Winnie Mandela's late sister, looks on.

◀▌ Undisguised joy at being together again. Walter Sisulu shares a joke with Archbishop Desmond and Leah Tutu in the garden of the Mandela home. Saturday, 17 February 1990.

◄■ Renewing an old friendship. Nelson Mandela entertains Advocate George Bizos, veteran political defence lawyer.

■► Mandela, aged 71, a free man after 26 years as a political prisoner.

◄■ Mandela greets a member of the American ABC news team at his home in Soweto. *Nightline* anchorman Ted Koppel looks on.

<ID1> Nelson Mandela and photographer Alf Kumalo.

1333/88: NELSON MANDELA.

Dear Alf,

I thank you for the photographs and inspiring message. I only hope that I will be able, in due course, to thank you face to face for this unexpected gesture. Meantime, I send you and your family fond regards and best wishes.

        Sincerely,
        Nelson, Zaenily & family

Victor Verster Prison,
Private Bag X 6005,
Paarl South.

LEST WE FORGET ...

This book is dedicated to my parents, **Mbube and Dolly Kumalo,** and to all those comrades who have given their lives to the struggle — those who have died in its cause and those who continue to work towards peace in South Africa.

A C K N O W L E D G E M E N T S   Over the years and during the making of this book, many people have given me support, encouragement and assistance. Grateful thanks to my family, especially my grandmother, Dikane Kumalo, my brothers Kaizer, Len, Dumisane and my sister Rose. To Can Themba, who encouraged me to produce a book as far back as the '60s. To Harvey Tyson, John Pitts and Ron Anderson of *The Star* for help received and permission to reproduce in the book pictures used by the newspaper. To Winnie and Zindzi Mandela, Desmond Tutu, Joel Mervis, Joe Thloloe, Aggrey Klaaste, Montsioa Moroke and Sol Makgabutlane. To Herbert Mabuza who helped with printing and Nomthetho Simelane who filed more than a thousand negatives. To Anton Sassenberg and Shane Hartdegen of Press Books, for turning the words and pictures into a book, Beulah Thumbadoo for research and Alison Lowry for co-ordinating the project. To Maud Motanyane of *Tribute* magazine for her constant encouragement and for permission to use the photograph of Prof Mphahlele on the cover.